Doing Greek Philosophy

CW00820304

Doing Greek Philosophy conveys a vivid sense of the dynamism and continuity in the Greek philosophical tradition and shows how interaction between Greek philosophers creates and sustains that tradition. It concentrates on a set of interrelated challenges and problems which come to light early in the tradition, and moves on to subsequent reactions to these issues. Throughout attention is paid not only to what these Greek philosophers were doing, but also to what they thought they were doing, since philosophy must have a sense of itself. Thus the goal is not just to inform readers about the fundamentals of Greek philosophy but also to equip them with a sort of intellectual toolkit, and encourage them to start using it. Readers will be left with a number of good philosophical questions and advised to pursue them further.

Robert Wardy is Reader in Ancient Philosophy and teaches classics and philosophy at St Catharine's College, the University of Cambridge. His publications include books and articles on both ancient western philosophy and Chinese language and culture.

Classical Foundations

The books in this series introduce students to the broad areas of study within classical studies and ancient history. They will be particularly helpful for students coming to the subject for the first time, or to those already familiar with an academic discipline who need orientation in a new field. The authors work to a common brief but not to a rigid structure: they set out to demonstrate the importance of the chosen subject and the lines of recent and continuing research and interpretation. Each book will provide a brief survey of the range of the subject, accompanied by some case studies demonstrating how one may go deeper into it. Each will also include guidance of a practical kind on sources, resources and reference material, and how to pursue the subject further. When complete, the series will comprise a critical map of the whole field of ancient studies.

The series is planned to include:

Early Christianity
Greek History
Greek Literature
Greek Philosophy
Late Antiquity
Latin Literature
Roman Social History
The Roman Empire

Books currently available in the series:

Roman Social History
Susan Treggiari

Greek History
Robin Osborne

Latin Literature
Susanna Morton Braund

Doing Greek Philosophy
Robert Wardy

Doing Greek Philosophy

Robert Wardy

LONDON AND NEW YORK

First published 2006
by Routledge
2 Park Square, Milton Park, Abingdon, Oxon OX14 4RN

Simultaneously published in the USA and Canada
by Routledge
270 Madison Ave, New York, NY 10016

Routledge is an imprint of the Taylor & Francis Group

© 2006 Robert Wardy

Typeset in Times by
Taylor & Francis Books
Printed and bound in Great Britain by
Antony Rowe Ltd, Chippenham, Wiltshire

British Library Cataloguing in Publication Data
A catalogue record for this book is available from the British Library

Library of Congress Cataloging in Publication Data
A catalog record for this book has been requested

ISBN10 0–415–28234–9   ISBN13 9–780–415–28234–5 (hbk)
ISBN10 0–415–28235–7   ISBN13 9–780–415–28235–2 (pbk)

Taylor & Francis Group is the Academic Division of T&F Informa plc.

Contents

Preface

Although I have been studying ancient philosophy for many years, this is my first attempt at something designed for a non-specialist audience. Not that I consider such work unworthy; on the contrary, I have avoided it until now because I felt that I lacked the skills required to provide a good entry route into the subject which I love. Some readers may feel that all that has changed is that in accepting the kind and flattering invitation of Richard Stoneman to contribute to this series, I succumbed to an attack of hubris. If others do not, that will in large measure be due to the input I received from my friends and colleagues Nicholas Denyer, Stephen Makin, Malcolm Schofield and David Sedley, with whom it is always an unmitigated pleasure to do Greek philosophy. I owe an equal debt to the students of past years whom I have attempted to teach. MM McCabe provided generous encouragement at a crucial juncture, for which I am very grateful. If this book displays any style, much of it must be due to the editorial elegance and incisive wit of Mary Bjork; and if it is less opaque, much of the clarity is owing to the helpful demands of Robert Bjork. It was once customary to acknowledge the services of a spouse – almost invariably a wife – who provided cups of coffee, demonstrated forbearing patience with authorial distraction, etc. My wife did no such thing. She behaved as normal – that is to say, beautifully. She is not a philosopher. But were she to read this book with approval, then I should have achieved success, for I dedicate it to Laurel Delamater as a very small token of a very great love.

Introduction

Doing and living philosophy

Imagine that you are one of a group of students ambitious to attend university, or already there. A curious visitor approaches the group to ask why individuals in it plumped for one or another course. Forget about those who reply 'it will lead to a job', or 'both my uncles are doctors', or 'the exams are a piece of cake'; let's think about those who express an interest in the courses themselves, rather than easy success, the approval of friends and family, or financial rewards. One student says: 'I want to be a scientist, to discover what the world is and how it works, and maybe to figure out how to change it'. We easily catch her drift, since we believe that all manner of scientific theories count as first-rate knowledge of the world, and are aware that many scientific discoveries have led to practical inventions, such as modern medicines and weapons, which have certainly changed the world – for good or bad. Another student says: 'I want to be a historian, to understand how people lived, what happened, and why things were so. Maybe my studies will even help me to understand what will happen, and advise politicians about how to get things right'. We're not surprised, since we're familiar with attempts to ascertain, explain and extrapolate from historical facts. A third student says: 'I want to study literature, to appreciate how it achieves its effects, and what makes for literary excellence. I also have writerly ambitions, and maybe a critical training will improve my own efforts'. Again this is familiar stuff, since we recognise that getting to grips with Milton or Joyce requires expertise. Finally, the visitor finds out that your aspiration is to become a philosopher. Now we're not sure what to think. Some of us have nearly been reduced to tears by pub bores who declare 'I've got a philosophy . . . ', and broadcast unwelcome views on anything ranging from how to seduce someone easily to the sinister manipulation of the stockmarket by extraterrestrials. That sort of 'philosophy' is nothing more than a label for supposedly privileged information about supposedly important matters, usually crackpot, and often fanatically espoused. But we think better of you than that – so what do you mean by 'philosophy'?

Perhaps you're the type who browses in bookshops, and have been intrigued by some of the material you've sampled in the philosophy section – especially a few dialogues by Plato, and other examples of ancient Greek philosophy. The visitor: 'We'll come to why what you dipped into was so attractive as to fix your university ambitions – not a trivial decision! But if you don't mind, there's a question I'd like to settle first. It's true that apart from second-hand bookstalls, where everything's lying about at random, these shops do organise their wares for good practical reasons. Although a decent number of customers will come in looking for a given book or, perhaps, something by a given author, and a very few haven't the foggiest idea of what they might buy, many people fall in between: they are looking for a particular kind of book, but nothing more specific than that. For example, I'm in the mood for a thriller – any decent thriller I haven't already read. Thus it's common sense for the clerk to be able to direct me to a section where I might find something which will take my fancy. But who decides what is shelved where? The easiest cases are practical guides (travel, etc.); biographies, and such like; technical textbooks; so-called "genre" fiction (romance, science fiction . . .); poetry, perhaps. But even these easiest cases aren't necessarily all that easy. It is usual to segregate "literature" from "genre" fiction – apparently the former is fancier, for the serious reader, and much more likely to be considered fit for academic study. However, plenty of prestigious authors have tried their hands at producing versions of "genre" fiction: where should such books go? To play it safe, the bookseller might place copies in several sections, and, of course, you can always ask at the information desk. That deals with the practical problem of laying your hands on a book: but what about the theoretical problem of figuring out what the book *is*? Which brings me to the point at issue. I'm a bookworm myself, and have browsed your favourite section: it's a rum lot. Apart from Plato, I found books of formal logic: why's that philosophy? They were full of symbols and equations: isn't that mathematics? And while some shops have separate "philosophy" and "mysticism" or "New Age" sections, others have a single "philosophy" collection which includes the favourites of our pub bores, whom we hoped we'd left behind. So you see, never mind whether the shops' layout is fine for rough and ready commercial purposes, I'm still not satisfied that we even know what we're talking about, let alone whether you're well-advised to embark on "philosophy"'.

You're not non-plussed. 'Yes, I noticed that myself. So I checked out the websites of several university faculties of philosophy, where they posted undergraduate reading lists. These certainly weren't identical – at one place a thinker named Heidegger was required reading, at another someone named Quine; and where Heidegger has to be done, Quine isn't even an option, and *vice versa*. But some names – for example, Plato's – seemed to crop up everywhere. So I'm confident that I can identify at least a core of texts which count as "philosophy"; the philosophy I'll get to study at university.' The visitor: 'Fair enough. But excuse me – why should I be impressed with these self-proclaimed university "philosophers"? Doubtless their professional classifications aren't the same as the booksellers', but until I learn what principles they use to mark out their discipline, I'm not satisfied that you're coping with the predicament. In other words, tell me, what *is* philosophy?'

Now you're beginning to feel hard-pressed: why is the visitor giving you such a tough time? But you have an answer. 'On one of the websites, I read "philosophy is the study of fundamental problems about the nature of knowledge and reality, and about our moral and political ideas"; so that's what's special about it.' It doesn't any longer come as a complete surprise that the visitor isn't satisfied. 'Oh, really? "The study of fundamental problems about the nature of knowledge and reality" sounds awfully like our first friend, the scientist; and "our moral and political ideas" would seem to be the business of our second friend, the historian. I know of properly cohesive combined courses, such as physics and chemistry taken together. But why on earth put a kind of science and a kind of history together?' By now you're not sure why you should submit to such a grilling, but don't like the idea of just walking away: what sort of fool wants to study something, and can't even say what it is? And you do have a come-back. 'But there was something more: they said that "in universities philosophy is studied in a way which lays considerable emphasis on very precise and careful argument". So I'll be different from the others, because there will be lots of argument, and the arguing will draw the subject together.' At last this elicits a smile from the stranger. 'Very good. But tell me: don't scientists and historians argue about their problems, and for their solutions? And I'm sure that our budding critic won't accept the notion that anything goes; literary critics have their reasons, and argue over interpretations. So, if you're on to something, it must be because philosophers engage in special kinds of arguments, or maybe argue in a special way. Thus it seems that in order to address our question, "what *is* philosophy?", we must first get straight on argument. Tell me: what *is* an argument?'

It's getting late; looking around, you realise that the others have drifted off some time ago, and there seems to be no satisfying this man; but still, the intellectual pressure of his probing, if taxing, isn't tedious. 'You win. I guess that not any old discussion counts as an "argument" – but I don't know what more to say. I mean, I had a real row with my parents about whether I could go away for the weekend; and I heard the other students arguing about whether science or history does more for people. I can't say what makes these disagreements "arguments", or whether they were good arguments (my parents won). I can't say whether all disagreements are arguments, or whether all arguments are disagreements. I *do* want to do philosophy; although I have to admit that sounds like I want to do something, but don't know what it is I want to do – and that's foolish. But hang on: how could I even get into such a weird state of mind?'

'Yes, if you put it that way, there is at least a whiff of paradox about it. And that you are troubled is a good sign. Now I have a confession to make. I'm a philosophical visitor, and the discussion we've been having is philosophy, or close to it. So don't worry too much, you're already doing what you want to do, know it or not![1] Let me help you out a bit. For sure we say that people screaming abuse at one another "are having an argument"; but that's importantly different from trying to solve a problem or settle a dispute by marshalling reasons on one side or the other, and assessing their relative merits. Other people at university – and elsewhere, everywhere! – "argue" in this latter sense. The thing – or anyway *a* thing – that's special about philosophy is that it's oddly reflexive. I mean that philosophers not only present and evaluate reasons, they also characteristically reflect on what makes for a good argument, they argue about what argument is, or should be.

And by the way, I let your friends off some philosophical hooks because they didn't seem that way inclined. I could have asked the first: "I suppose you'll do some lab work, to find out what causes what. Imagine you've conducted an experiment, with such-and-such a result. Experiments have to be 'controlled': that is, the conditions must be such as to ensure that you've isolated factors really responsible for the effect. But if you tell me that you checked to make sure the apparatus wasn't dirty, how do you know that your inspection wasn't faulty? Where are the proper limits of experimental justification? And anyway, you're making an extrapolation: that set-ups like this one will have similar effects; why should we assume that like regularly causes like?" And I could have pressed the second, also on causation: "If I'm puzzled about this scientist's procedure, your situation seems more dubious. Difficult as it might be to understand the doings of carbon or electrons, the behaviour of material stuffs doesn't display variety or complexity remotely approaching the intricacy of human interactions; and life doesn't throw up plentiful opportunities for conducting anything like an experiment which would put a historical conjecture to the test. So how be confident that a science of humanity is even possible?" And I could have put the third on the spot: "There's an old saying – *de gustibus non disputandum*, there's no arguing over taste. Why shouldn't anything go in literature? What makes for objective literary judgements, as opposed to bald subjective preferences?" You'll find that it is possible to study the philosophy of science, the philosophy of history, aesthetics . . . As a matter of fact, reflection on categories and taxonomy might also generate an interesting conversation with a philosophically-minded bookseller. So you see, we're better off conceiving of philosophy as a special approach to problems, rather than as defined by the problems themselves. This formal approach to our focal question has a pleasing consequence, that everybody's business can be the philosopher's business, because we dig down to the unexamined presuppositions of the way they go on.

Now that's only the beginnings of a rudimentary answer; I've done little more than give you a few illustrations, and haven't started arguing about the nature of argument. And philosophers being what they are, were I to do that, some would no doubt hotly dispute my results. Some would even deny that argument is essential to the business; but I think that if they *argued* with me, it wouldn't be too hard to embarrass them; and if they consistently refused to argue for their position, we could rightly dismiss them as "philosophers" in scare-quotes. So we have ever so much work to do; but I can assure you that we have started working.

I haven't forgotten that you said Greek philosophy particularly interested you. That might seem wildly eccentric, if you want to *do* philosophy; in fact, some of my colleagues distinguish sharply between philosophy itself, and the history of philosophy. I myself work on ancient philosophy, and maintain that I'm a philosopher for all that. So I had better explain the reasons for surprise or scepticism about this claim, and attempt to dismantle them.

The sceptic about the *philosophical* study of Greek philosophy might object: "That first friend of yours is in proper intellectual order. Contrast her with a crazy mate who starts off by expressing the same aspirations, but then declares that he wishes to become a practising alchemist, to explore the natural world clinging to beliefs and deploying techniques which have long since been entirely discredited. That's a mad scientist in the making. Or consider a milder eccentric whose self-imposed limitation is to become expert in pre-Einsteinian physics: if some of his theory and practice does remain current, isn't it nevertheless sheer perversity not to take advantage of all the best available? And the best will be up to date. True, there are, say, athletes who might attempt to scale a Himalayan peak without oxygen, or row across the Atlantic single-handed, but science isn't a game. In sport we are free to define the challenges of a contest, and set out to overcome them with minimal resources; handicaps are a source of pride. But in science we seek to minimise what baffles our understanding, since the obstacles nature presents are more than formidable enough on their own. And what goes for science holds good of philosophy too. I concede that history is a reputable academic discipline; but just as historians of science are historians, not scientists, so historians of philosophy are historians – not philosophers".

This case seems plausible enough; but let us examine its merits, to see whether it is really partially or even completely specious. It holds water to the extent that philosophers really are scientists, or relevantly similar to them. And some examples of philosophical work strongly suggest that this is so. Close to the beginning of philosophy in Greece, Parmenides declared that it is impossible to think or speak of what is not. He is indeed a philosopher, since he sought to establish this denial by way of rigorous argument. Just what he meant, and what his argument was, are not our present concern. For simplicity's sake, consider this little argument, after Parmenides: "whenever I think – say, of you – or speak – perhaps I comment that the weather is fine – there is something or other which I think or utter. For how could it be otherwise? To claim that I am thinking – of nothing – would be to contradict myself. Speech and thought require objects, and *nothing* is not an object". There is indeed a deep puzzle here. Something along these lines seems impossible to deny, but, on the other hand, I am experiencing no difficulty in thinking about my dead grandmother, who is no longer, or Mr Pickwick, who never was. And a feature of ancient Greek produces another twist, since in that language it is idiomatic to refer to falsehood as "what is not"; therefore a speaker of that language unable to resist the force of Parmenidean arguments would have to admit that falsehood seems to be impossible, that to speak is automatically to speak the truth. But, of course, we all too easily get things wrong, or maliciously tell lies. In his dialogue the *Sophist*, Plato makes his most sustained attack on the problem of the (im)possibility of falsehood; his solution turns on distinguishing between that of which we are thinking or speaking, and what we think about it. For example, I might entertain the false thought that you are flying about the room; and, in ancient Greek, that would be an instance of "thinking what is not". So how is it that this is not impossibly thinking, but thinking of nothing? Well, I *am* thinking of something – you, but what I think about you, flying, is not one of your properties. This is fine, so far as it goes. But Plato's solution is limited: it fails to address the issue of how we might meaningfully think or speak of "what is not" in the sense of what does not exist. About two and a half millennia after Plato, Bertrand Russell proposed a solution to such puzzles. Very roughly put, it goes something like this: were I to say "the girl in the next room has red hair", and there's no girl in there, it sounds as if I'm impossibly describing someone who isn't around to have hair of any shade; how then can my words have meaning, if there simply is no one around for them to be about? Russell proposes that my statement is logically more complicated than appears on the surface: what it really comes to is approximately "there is a girl in the next room; she has red hair". Since the first component of the statement is false, the second has no application, it falls void.[2]

Many others have proposed or modified theories of language which seek to account for our ability to miss the truth, and to make our ability to conceive of what does not exist (relatively) unmysterious. When one reviews this work, a conclusion which readily recommends itself is that philosophical logic is a unified enterprise, unified because it addresses fixed *explananda*. And, where one has a research agenda, contributions to it are up for comparative assessment; there is, or can be, objective progress. This sounds very like science. Often (but not invariably) earlier contributions to the research programme will strike us as having been of real merit in their place and at their time, but later work, as it advances, improves on them, often replacing them altogether. Plato on falsehood is the stuff of history, not living philosophy; and so it seems that the allegedly *philosophical* student of Greek philosophy is indeed uncomfortably like the mad scientist, or at best the perversely self-handicapped one, rather than the sober historian of science.

To repeat, this holds water to the extent that philosophers really are scientists, or relevantly similar to them; but much, maybe most, philosophy is not really like my highly simplified sketch of a fragment of philosophical logic. There are a number of reasons for this state of affairs. Philosophers of the highest reputation are and always have been locked in disagreement over what the really important problems are; and even when they agree on this score, they are very prone to differ profoundly over how such problems are to be handled. So instead of encountering a group of nicely unified research programmes, we find a plethora of intellectual episodes which do often hang together internally as their participants argue with and against one another, but precious few larger integrated patterns. For the sceptical critique to be sustained, one would have to dismiss out of hand a huge amount of what is palpably significant philosophy. Furthermore, a great many topics seem to lack the "scientific" contours visible in logic and some other areas. To take just the most obvious example, argumentative ethics is most certainly philosophical. To put the point abstractly, theories of who we are and might or should aspire to become are surely constrained by facts about humanity, and some of these facts come within the purview of science. But within such necessary constraints philosophers freely speculate in a manner irreducible to one or another agenda; all over the place we discover philosophical activity which does not fall into neat temporal sequences wherein "later" is more likely than not to mean "better". Much Greek philosophy is of this kind.

There you have some sort of response to my sceptical colleague. There is a great deal more to say, on both his side and mine; and what I have said is sketchy in the extreme. But you and I have made a start; I do hope you persevere, and maybe even come to work with me.'

That is the end of my make-believe inquisition. I am now going to expand on some of its implications *in propria persona*, with a view to explaining what this book will try to accomplish. To begin with, since the topic is Greek philosophy, it will be in order to think harder about what it means to be engaged in the study of the history of philosophy. And here we can afford not to jump in immediately as partisans of the visitor against his hostile colleague (although I am by profession a student of Greek philosophy, and you wouldn't be my reader unless you have at least a passing interest in the subject). All historians mine the past, but there are strikingly different motivations for so doing, beyond simply establishing what was what (and since all history beyond the most elementary chronicling inevitably involves interpretation, things swiftly become anything but simple). We can start with a medical analogy, although it won't get us very far. Just as it still happens that some remedy known to, for example, Amazonian Indians can be exploited by our doctors, so too study of the medicine of the past has, on occasion, brought to light treatments of interest to modern medical science. Analogously, might not the philosophy of the past reveal ideas and arguments subsequently forgotten or unfairly overlooked? There is something in this analogy, but left unqualified it betrays a much too unsophisticated conception of philosophy. In the medical case, we might investigate the properties of some plant extract which was used to treat one or another malady, and establish that it really is beneficial; never mind that our source believes that it taps into some demonic healing power, while we repose our confidence in biochemical trials. What holds constant is that they and we alike want to cure bellyache, and this remedy works: the painful symptoms haven't changed over time, and everyone wants to feel better. With rare and rather abstruse exceptions, philosophy isn't like that. While it is indeed a special activity – Greek or mediaeval philosophers are indubitably *philosophers* – philosophy is practised in a socio-historical context, and its practitioners react in manifold ways, conscious and unconscious, to the shaping influences of when and where they live. Thus, except for those rare and usually technical results, it does not happen that some past insight can be unearthed 'as is' and put to use within a contemporary debate; the very terms in which the debates of the here and now are cast are often not those current in other places and at other times. Philosophy has taken place in divergent conceptual environments.

Let us accordingly consider two contrasting examples. Until quite recently, philosophical ethics was largely dominated by argument between proponents of so-called deontological and consequentialist theories: the former take as fundamental the concept of right action, the latter regard good states of affairs as basic. The arguments concern whether actions really can be shown to be prior to states of affairs or *vice versa*, and, within each tendency, how best to analyse (in)correct action, what makes a state of affairs good or how to increase goodness, and so forth. But 'virtue ethics' has emerged on the scene; its proponents focus on the concept of agency, and how we might best characterise a virtuous agent.[3] Many of its champions take their inspiration from ancient ethical theories, especially those of Aristotle. And it is true that these theories are preoccupied with working out what makes for a good human life, and what human beings must be like in order to achieve success. As you would expect, the differences between Aristotle and a modern virtue theorist are many and important, but they are both virtue theorists, and it is a matter of fact that reading the ancients has, in this case, fed into modern ethics fairly directly. This example speaks in favour of the medical analogy.

But then again, consider the philosophy of mind. In his work *De Anima* (*On the Soul*), Aristotle argues that mind and body are neither identical nor two separate things somehow related to one another; rather mind (or most of it) and body are distinct aspects of the living animal; and the soul is something like a set of organisational principles and nested capacities which endow the animal with the ability to live its life. Until several decades ago, the philosophy of mind was largely dominated by argument between materialists and dualists: the former identify the mind with some part of the body (usually the brain, or parts of it), the latter regard the mind as an immaterial thing distinct from the body. The arguments concern such issues as whether a physical thing could have subjective or conscious experiences (a problem for materialists), whether there could be causal interaction between something immaterial and matter (a problem for dualists), and so forth. Then 'functionalism' sprang up. Functionalists argue that the very question 'mind and body: one thing or two?' is ill-posed; rather, having a mind consists in one or another type of matter (not necessarily the same kind of matter) being so organised as to react to stimuli in the ways which animals do. And prominent functionalists have argued that Aristotle's view of the soul as an organisational principle and set of capacities is a sort of functionalism before the letter, and claimed him as a venerable ancestor. However, some experts in

Greek philosophy have rejected this genealogy, arguing that Aristotle's conception of matter and perceptual processes is so radically unlike ours that his philosophy of mind is truly alien; the appearances are misleading, and Aristotelian philosophy of mind is an antique, not to be re-conditioned for current philosophical use.[4] I have been won over by the anti-functionalists. The debate is an intricate one and unresolved; but it is uncontentious that plenty of other examples of past assumptions, arguments and doctrines flatly incompatible with what is accepted in modern philosophy are there to take its place, if required. These examples speak against the medical analogy.

Aristotelian philosophy of mind is fascinating, a thing of beauty; my message is not to dismiss it as a worthless relic! So you might recur to the earlier compare-and-contrast exercise: maybe the historian of philosophy is related not only to the political or social historian, but also to the literary critic? After all, whatever criteria critics use to select those texts which they regard as interesting or profitable or amusing to study, they do not include being 'up to date'; literary fashions do change, but only to change again. There is a similarity to be found here, since philosophers take aesthetic delight in ingenious and subtle arguments (as mathematicians admire elegant proofs), but the difference is more important. You will remember the visitor remarking that aesthetics reflects on the nature and qualities of literary artefacts; and whether and how works of fiction, although false (these things never happened, or not in this way; these people never existed, or, if they did, did not think these thoughts, etc.), might nevertheless convey important truths or deliver significant insights, as many people believe, are outstanding philosophical puzzles. So we need not insist that literature does not deal in truth. However, the manner in which fiction embodies or suggests truths, if indeed it does, is utterly distinct from philosophy's relation to truth (by the way, philosophers try to define and understand truth itself). For all real philosophers are aiming at the truth, by means of the best arguments at their disposal.

It immediately follows that historians of philosophy have no choice but to adopt a critically engaged stance to their objects of study. We read Aristotle or Descartes in order to understand them. To understand them, we must analyse their arguments. But to analyse their arguments is to evaluate them, since this is work intended to establish truths on the basis of correct reasoning, and hence cannot be approached other than critically. Logicians distinguish between 'valid' and 'sound' arguments. Here are some intuitive examples to illustrate the distinction. (1) 'If you have shut the door, it is closed; but the door is closed; so you shut it.' That is invalid. (2) 'If you have shut the door, it is closed; but you shut it; so the door is closed.' That is valid. Where is the difference? If Y follows from X, and if X is true, so too is Y; but we cannot infer that Y's truth suffices to establish X's, since we have not shown that the *only* way for Y to be true is if X is true (maybe someone else shut the door). And what makes for soundness? That (2) is valid does not guarantee that the door is closed. 'If you have shut the door, it is closed': yes, so long as no one else subsequently opened it, etc. 'But you shut it': did you? If Y follows from X, and X *is* true, so too is Y.[5] Sometimes the historian of philosophy's engagement with past work might make available sound reasoning (perhaps virtue ethics?); and sometimes that engagement might clarify reasoning which is valid, but not, we think, sound (perhaps portions of Aristotelian philosophy of mind?). And, of course, we often come to the conclusion that the arguments we study are invalid (not that this *ipso facto* robs them of interest: give me a challenging but flawed piece of reasoning rather than an acceptable but dull one every time). But any which way, historians of philosophy are engaged. And that shows that, although they might have some things in common with literary critics, there is also a vital difference. Remember that the third student was not sure that pursuing literary studies would connect up with writing some fiction of his own: rightly so, since to study literature is not to write literature (not that that excludes some sort of connection – consider that, for example, stretching is not running, but warming up will improve your performance on the track). But since the only legitimate stance for the historian of philosophy to adopt is one of critical engagement, which entails the scrupulous dissection of arguments, to do the *history* of philosophy is to do *philosophy*.

So we discern some merit on both sides in the disagreement between the visitor and his sceptical colleague. On the one hand, philosophical historians are doing philosophy, with one another and, in a peculiar way, with the dead. What I mean is this: in daily life we all routinely engage in hypothetical reasoning. Either by ourselves or in the company of others, we take as true some beliefs to which we are not in fact committed, or even beliefs which we actually reject. Why? I don't know whether you did well in an exam, but don't want to ask straight out in case you were disappointed and my question will upset you. I take you out for coffee and observe your behaviour. I reason: 'Suppose she did well; since the exam is important to her, success would make itself apparent in her behaviour. But she sat there slumped into her chair, staring in a gloomy and distracted fashion, and a smile never crossed her face – oh dear, it did not go well'. Here there is something I do not know; I hypothesise its truth, discover that the facts are inconsistent with the hypothesis, and so reject it. Or I ascertain that you are keen on improving your appearance through cosmetic surgery. Together we engage in a lively discussion of the pros and cons of your signing up for a new nose or for collagen injections first, and look into which surgeon should be approached. It so happens that I consider cosmetic surgery repugnant and often dangerous, but I am capable of assuming true some beliefs (e.g. 'it would be good for you to acquire big, pouty lips') which I actually reject, and reasoning as if they were true. Such suppositional reasoning is immensely valuable in a host of academic disciplines, mathematical, scientific and philosophical.

In the case in hand, when we do philosophy with a Greek philosopher, we ascertain as best we can what he believes to be true and try to work out whether the positions he adopts can be reached by valid arguments from these beliefs, whether or not we share them. Nothing follows immediately concerning the worth or interest of this philosophy. Sometimes we already share or come to share these beliefs, and might accept the results *in propria persona*. Sometimes we remain uncommitted either way. Sometimes we reject them. This last case breaks down into a number of possibilities. It can happen that although I think that what you believe is false, I can see that it is rational and intelligent for you to be mistaken; I might say to myself, 'were I in her position, I'd be thinking the same way; and her thinking is very clever'. Or not: either because the falsehoods to which you subscribe are fatuous or bizarre, or because your arguments, never mind what is held true, are boring or awful. Of course, I am fallible; just as I might be mistaken about the exam (it went wonderfully well, but you're downcast because your mother is ill), so too my verdict concerning the commitments of a Greek philosopher and how well he develops them might be in error. But the job is to do our level best, to ascribe to him what we consider the best possible beliefs and arguments consistent with the evidence.

This matter of the need for consistency with the evidence reveals the merit on the side of the sceptical colleague. I am suggesting that doing the history of philosophy is like engaging in argument with absent partners, conducting an imaginary dialogue wherein we keep up both sides of the conversation. But we are not at liberty to say whatever we like: Parmenides' surviving words preclude ascribing to him certain arguments for the impossibility of thinking of what is not; Aristotle is manifestly committed to the ethnic superiority of the Greeks. If I work with a living philosopher, our only constraints are our intelligence, knowledge, originality and good will; if I work on a dead philosopher, I am obliged to respect what I know or believe he believed, and the dead do not change their minds. One might push harder. 'All too often, the surviving evidence for Greek philosophy is exiguous. We believe that Empedocles posited a cosmic cycle; but what survives of his writing is indeterminate between rival and incompatible reconstructions of that cycle. Wouldn't it be nice if we could simply put the question to him? Similarly, some of us believe that Aristotle's philosophy evolved over time, others are sure that it constitutes a single and fairly static system: he could have said, but sadly didn't. Your job as a historian is to produce the most plausible interpretations, consistent with the ascertainable facts; and if I concede that that will entail engaging in hypothetical philosophy in the way you've described, it surely will also involve doing work which is not philosophy, on *your* conception of philosophy.'

This should be happily conceded; but it amounts to the concession that studying the history of philosophy is a hybrid activity embracing a set of cooperative skills. And one should not concede too much. While it is true that our knowledge of Greek philosophers would make enormous advances, were we to have a fuller written record, let alone miraculously bring them back to life, the identification and assessment of philosophy is regularly a most opaque affair. This can be seen at once if one reflects on what can happen in discussion amongst contemporary philosophers. True, it does happen that philosopher *B* feels that philosopher *A* is committed to this or that for these reasons; *A* acknowledges as much; and *B* poses a question or urges an objection which *A* answers or meets, to *B*'s (dis)satisfaction. But quite often it isn't like that: *A* might feel that *B* simply can't get him right, never mind see where he is open to questioning or objection; more radically, *A* might even have a less than completely firm grip on the nature of her own commitments. How could that be? Wouldn't this lack of self-knowledge be a terrible indictment of her philosophical credentials? Not necessarily. Since argument is the stuff of philosophy, and tracing out the full implications of tricky arguments requires much talent and finesse, it is entirely possible that a creator of or adherent to a philosophical theory lacks awareness of some of its implications – even of crucial ones. This injects some real indeterminacy into what is believed, and why. Living philosophical debate is fluid and dynamic, as arguments are clarified, modified, abandoned. Historical interpretation obviously lacks this flexibility; however, it is not cut and dried, since as we work with our imaginary partners, we too enjoy considerable leeway to adjust our suppositions, within the limits of all the evidence available to us.

Two things to avoid at all cost. First, we are not to be 'Whiggish' historians, certain that the history of philosophy is a history of linear progress; we have seen some of the reasons this cannot be so. Second, it is sometimes said that the proper way to approach the philosophy of the past should not be by way of doing philosophy; rather, this is rightly undertaken through explication and analysis which, for the sake of objectivity, strictly abjures argumentative engagement (some, but not all, so-called 'history of ideas' is like this). This is and must be incorrect. I don't mean that to approach philosophy non-philosophically need be improper (e.g. there is obviously nothing disreputable in studying how some philosophical positions might have influenced works of art, say Platonism's influence on Shelley or Schopenhauer's on Wagner). But if our case for the inevitability of critical engagement was a good one, then the best possible objective interpretations are always elucidation and evaluation at once.

So much for thinking harder about what it means to be engrossed in the history of philosophy in general; now for Greek philosophy, and what we shall be doing with it in particular. This is philosophy: what is importantly 'Greek' about it? You might have noticed that I have referred indifferently to 'Greek philosophy', 'ancient philosophy', 'ancient Greek philosophy'. Such variation is acceptable common practice. First, as to the 'Greek' variant: although this tradition survived unbroken right down until the end of antiquity, and thus throughout both the pagan and Christian Roman eras, philosophy under the Roman empire remained an activity which was, and was perceived to be, 'Greek' in character. Although, of course, philosophers reacted in important ways to the circumstances in which they lived, most philosophers were of Greek origin; later ancient philosophy was deeply bedded in earlier Greek work; nearly all philosophers knew the Greek language,[6] and even the great majority of those who were not ethnic Greeks and did not speak Greek as a first language wrote in Greek (virtually all Latin philosophical texts are peppered with references to Greek work, while there is only a tiny number of Greek references to Latin work). This is not to denigrate the achievements of Roman philosophy, in which the contributions of Lucretius, Cicero and Seneca, all written in Latin, are outstanding and, in part, occupied with Roman concerns.[7] But they too avowedly build on very extensive Greek foundations; so we shall refer to '(ancient) Greek philosophy', taking our lead from the people who lived and saw it that way during Greco-Roman antiquity.

Second, as to the 'ancient' variant: is this to imply that the ancient cultures of China and India, to take the two most obvious examples, had no philosophy? Yes and no: to recur to an issue which has confronted us from the outset, it all depends on what you mean by 'philosophy'. If that word designates some body of privileged knowledge or wisdom concerning matters of great importance recognised as such, then it would be the most blinkered chauvinism to insist that this is a special Greek preserve. However, if that word designates the type of reflexive, self-aware argumentative activity we have been exploring, then its primary territory is indeed Greek. If you have heard of any Chinese 'philosopher', it will have been Confucius. But if you have read the work which goes under his name, known in the West as the *Analects*, you will not have noticed a significant quantity of argument. Much disagreement, and many lessons about who we are and how we ought to live, but Confucius is very seldom depicted as trying to persuade his interlocutors or followers through sustained, justified reasoning. He was dubbed '*the* Chinese philosopher' by the Jesuit missionaries who recognised his towering presence in China and applied their own categories to this alien culture; but this is a dangerous misrepresentation, since someone coming to Confucius expecting 'philosophy' as I have roughly defined it will be sorely disappointed, and tempted to form an unfavourable judgement of the Chinese. Thus to apply the term 'philosophy' in a relatively strict sense to the wisdom of ancient cultures beyond Greece is, if any-thing, to run the risk of unfair denigration. This is clearly not to imply that 'philosophy' is an honorific which trumps all else. And there are Chinese thinkers whose major persuasive and debating strategies really are 'philosophical' to the core. The best example is the later followers of someone named Mo Tzu, whose pre-occupation with argument led to the development of semantic and logical theory. However, in all likelihood you will never have heard of Mo Tzu and his followers; that is because their impact on Chinese culture was almost null.[8] All ancient peoples argued – all people argue. All ancient peoples produced what they regarded as wisdom – and such wisdom deserves our respect and amply repays study. Some non-Greek ancient people were most certainly doing philosophy. But for an entire and vibrant tradi-tion, go to the Greeks.

I have been harping on about difference and exclusivity, and appropriately so. For I am taking a leaf from the book of Greek culture. From earliest times, the ancient Greeks set great stock by wisdom, the aspirants to which staked their claims by virtue of widely disparate kinds of expertise (political, military, religious, medical, literary . . .). And the commonplace that the Greeks were an exceptionally contentious, competitive and aggressive lot is correct (somewhat innocuously, this was an 'agonistic' culture). In such an atmosphere, one rightly anticipates that rival claimants to wisdom will represent themselves as not only in pos-session of special knowledge, but also as having acquired their insights in remarkable ways. No group went in for such self-differentiation more assiduously than philosophers. And in accordance with our model, the very first philosophers not only argued robustly, they also argued about what makes for a good argument. The most widely used Greek term for 'reasoning' or 'argument' is *logos*: very soon the philosophers were claiming – on the basis of *logos* – that they had a special way of producing, refining and defending good *logos*.

This argumentative work was anything but a solitary activity. Greek philosophers constantly engaged in lively, often fierce debate, the word for which is 'dialectic' ('dialectic' is simply a transliteration of a term of art of Greek philosophy). This fact has wide-reaching repercussions on how Greek philosophy must be studied. Greek philosophers were stimulated not only by their contemporaries, but also formed into more or less (in)formal chronological lineages; at one, minimal extreme, reading and reacting to predecessors, at the other, maximal one, becoming members of fully fledged, institutionalised 'schools' supplying philosophical curricula fed by an elaborate inheritance of intra- and inter-school debate. Greek philosophy is traditional, through and through; although the history of philosophy contains numerous cohesive periods, nothing comes close to matching the glorious unification of the Greek tradition.[9] Living Greek philosophers engaged in dialectical argument with those who came before. A surprising and pleasant result follows from this. Earlier I spoke of conducting an imaginary dialogue wherein we keep up both sides of the conversation, when we do the history of philosophy philosophically. It now emerges that when the ancient Greeks themselves were doing philosophy, their traditional conception of the activity involved them in doing much the same thing. Of course that tradition is now a thing of the past, and it would be crazy to aspire to becoming a Greek philosopher. However, it turns out that historians of Greek philosophy proceed in a fashion which is much more than superficially related to the procedures of those they study: ancient work is the inception of (the history of) philosophy – which is the justification for this book's title.

Now a negative bit about what this book is not. It is neither a handbook nor a wide-reaching historical survey. There are a number of reasons for this. First, there already exist many such books covering individual Greek philosophers, schools and historical periods; some of them are excellent,[10] and it would be pointless to add to their number. Second, there is always the danger that a historical survey will not be doing Greek philosophy, that it will lapse into 'the history of ideas' in the pejorative sense of that phrase, slighting argument in the course of the bland summary of doctrines. Third, I shall provide the bare minimum of bibliography. Some of the excellent books I shall mention contain very full and up-to-date reading lists, and the intention is to help you do Greek philosophy, not passively to ingest other people's interpretations.

Now a positive bit about what this book is. As I have said, there is no pretension of comprehensive coverage. But I am very concerned to convey a vivid sense of the dynamism and continuity of the Greek philosophical tradition, how interaction between Greek philosophers creates and sustains that tradition. Therefore we shall concentrate on a set of interrelated challenges and problems which come to light early in the tradition, and move on to subsequent reactions to these issues. Sometimes the links will be very direct, a later philosopher explicitly arguing with an earlier one. Sometimes the connections will be real but implicit and thematic, established by mapping out how alternative positions on some of these issues which partially define the tradition came to be adopted. Throughout we shall pay attention not only to what these Greek philosophers were doing, but also to what they thought they were doing, since philosophy must have a sense of itself. Thus the goal is not to make you someone who 'knows (a bit) about' Greek philosophy, but rather to equip you with a sort of intellectual toolkit, and encourage you to start using it. The nature of the exercise entails that I am not at all anxious that you come away from your reading feeling 'these problems have been solved, these puzzles have been cracked' – indeed, the reverse. Of course I have selected a strand of the tradition which I regard as important, interesting and rewardingly difficult, with the consequence that definitive, final verdicts will not be forthcoming. The Greek word for a philosophical problem or puzzle is *aporia*; Aristotle (taking his cue from *Theaetetus* 155D) evocatively pronounces that philosophy begins in wonder. We shall be looking at the nature and significance of *aporia*, and this will be a fairly aporetic book. *Aporia* is a fine thing when it arises from there being two or more reasonably satisfying but mutually exclusive answers, rather than *no* satisfying answer at all – our puzzlement should be the encouraging kind, and you will be left with a budget of good philosophical questions, and advised on how to pursue them further.

Will you be fully equipped? No. You will be very much better placed than our imaginary student to build up your own collection of properly classified philosophical books. But a fully competent student of ancient philosophy needs plenty of historical and linguistic credentials to be able to appreciate and take account of the multifarious cultural factors which impinge on the philosophy. The preserved texts of what we have are often faulty and fragmentary, the language often difficult to understand; and much of it cannot be understood without sound knowledge of many features of ancient life, political, social, economic, material . . . In other words, the expert must be a trained classicist, as well as a philosopher. However, many philosophers who have lacked such expertise have nevertheless been able to participate at a very high level in the study of Greek philosophy (Aquinas' commentaries on Aristotle, to cite a rather impressive example). Working with translations and some background historical information, you can certainly participate actively (so long as you have a talent for philosophy!). If some of you are spurred on to consider acquiring the extra intellectual equipment, all the better.

To put some flesh on the bare bones of this description, before plunging in. We shall begin with the enigmatic philosopher Heraclitus. Heraclitus contended that if we listen to *the logos*, we shall come to learn that all things are one. What is this *logos*? Why is it authoritative, and what does that teach us about Heraclitus' view of philosophical reason? All things are one because the world (largely? entirely?) consists of structures whose components are opposites, in different kinds of opposition. In expressing this doctrine, Heraclitus seems to maintain a pair of startling theses: that what seems to be so is so – if at all – only from one limited perspective, among many from which it is not so; and, perhaps, that the world's oppositional structures are contradictory, in that the universal 'is and is not' conflicts are not, and cannot be, resolved. The first thesis brings to our attention the idea of 'relativism', that truths are not absolute, but rather true only relative to a given context. We shall supplement this relativistic material by inspecting the theological arguments of the philosopher Xenophanes, who developed an astonishing critique of conventional religious convictions which targeted their relativity to parochial beliefs and cultural assumptions. We shall also bring in Protagoras, portrayed in antiquity as the arch-champion of a far-reaching and subversive relativism. The second thesis will prompt us to ask: if Heraclitus did countenance or even embrace contradiction, can we make any sense of that? If unacceptable, is it plain false, or rather incoherent, 'incredible' in the strict sense of the word (viz *impossible* to believe)? Another memorable thesis is attributed to Heraclitus, the doctrine of flux, according to which all things 'flow', are in constant change. Inspection of this doctrine and its implications for identity will get us thinking along similar lines: never mind whether the world is in a state of radical flux, *could* it be, or is arguing for such a theory somehow self-defeating? The evidence for all three of these early Greek philosophers is sparse, incomplete and indirect; therefore we shall also have occasion to delve into how one goes about handling such evidence, and what the status of such historical reconstruction might be.

We continue with Plato's and Aristotle's antagonistic reactions to such philosophical positions. In his dialogue the *Theaetetus*, Plato represents Socrates investigating the question 'what is knowledge?' with some people named Theaetetus and Theodorus. (In many of the most famous dialogues, Socrates asks, concerning some important X, 'what is X?', and an argumentative, critical and frequently aporetic discussion ensues. The visitor of my little introductory dialogue is a very humble descendant of Socrates.) Theaetetus' first shot at an answer defines knowledge as perception, and the first part of the dialogue is a very complicated articulation, analysis and eventual refutation of this suggestion. We shall focus on a single aspect of this treatment. It seems obvious that many of our perceptions are false; in which case perception could not be knowledge, since knowledge is always of the truth. That would seem to put paid to Theaetetus' candidate definition, but Socrates comes to the rescue by invoking the doctrine of flux. We might speculate that if change really is radical and all-pervasive, then each and every perception might have the opportunity to hold true of one or another evanescent state of the world. But Socrates argues that there is a serious catch: if situations obtain so fleetingly as to preclude perceiving them falsely, might they not be so evanescent that our words cannot attach to them? So the *Theaetetus* questions the coherence of Heraclitus' thesis. And is this a fair attack on the historical Heraclitus? Socrates refers to the theory as a 'secret doctrine', which may be a signal that it is intended as an extrapolation from Heraclitean notions and arguments; in trying to gauge what is going on, we shall advance our project of studying how philosophical history is created. But Heraclitus is not the only past thinker to make an appearance in the *Theaetetus*. Socrates associates Heraclitus' flux with Protagoras' claim that all opinions are true; and the dialogue subjects its version of relativism to a series of objections, culminating in a purported self-refutation. Assessing some of these arguments will not only take us further into Greek reactions to relativism, but also further enhance our understanding of creative history: for Plato revives the dead Protagoras to speak on his own behalf. And since the *Theaetetus* shows us various interlocutors variously (un)committed to propositions to be attacked and defended, it also furnishes a superb case study of Greek dialectic as it happens. Or rather, what we read is not Plato in his own voice, but a philosophical drama whose characters are represented doing philosophy. Why is this Plato's chosen philosophical vehicle? Thinking about that will advance our project of exploring some of the different ways in which philosophy was done and presented in the ancient West.

Heraclitus and Protagoras (or Heracliteanism and Protagoreanism) stand accused of incoherence and of refuting themselves (on different grounds, although similar dialectical strategies are in play). In *Metaphysics Gamma*,[11] Aristotle accepts the Platonic pairing of Heraclitus with Protagoras, and accuses them of futilely trying to adopt positions which are untenable in a special sense: they literally cannot be occupied. This is because, on his analysis, their would-be doctrines wittingly or unwittingly seek to flout the principle of contradiction, which states that a proposition and another which contradicts it cannot be true simultaneously. The argument – which is obscure and difficult in the extreme, but very rewarding – concludes that such principles are so fundamental to all thought that, ironically, their defence against a misguided attempt to reject them is, in a subtle sense, question-begging, involving as it must do the very principles in question. Aristotle's discussion is a beautiful example of his version of dialectic. His way with an *aporia* is to marshal what he calls the relevant *endoxa* – reputable opinions – from all sorts of sources; put them into good order; see where they conflict, thus generating the *aporia*; run through anticipated objections; and finally solve the *aporia*. The solution is intended to preserve and go beyond what was right in his predecessors' and opponents' views. That is the ideal, from which Aristotle's practice often falls short. But no philosopher has ever used a more powerful and sophisticated technique, which will teach us a great deal about philosophical method and history.

The next stage will be to take another tack on puzzlement and how to cope with it, by turning to the ancient Sceptics. I capitalise 'Sceptics' to distinguish them from those who doubt some particular truth or body of truths, or, more generally, whose habit of mind is incredulous. In common usage, 'scepticism' can spring from all manner of causes, rational or irrational, and is not limited as to what it might concern (as in the imaginary sceptical colleague). I might be sceptical about how you will perform in your exams; I doubt that you will perform well. Why? I have it in for you; I have no good reason to doubt your scholastic ability or studious disposition, but tend irrationally to believe that my nasty desires will be satisfied. You might be sceptical about the current or future prospects for unified field theory; your doubts arise from intimate acquaintance with theoretical physics and rest on technical grounds. Unlike you, who are altogether confident about the outcome of the next national election, one of our friends is simply of a cautious cast of mind about any doubtful issue, having learnt how often our expectations prove rash in the event.

Ancient Sceptics are not to be identified with any of these common or garden-variety ones, although they resemble some more than others. The differences are rooted in the source and character of their outlook. Ancient philosophical Sceptics claim that there is no exit from *aporia*; not because we have not thought long or hard enough, but rather because either subjectively our cognitive resources can never cope with the puzzles, or objectively these puzzles are intrinsically impenetrable by any (human) mind. You might imagine that such an attitude is untenable: why ever should the rest of us optimistic philosophers concede that the Sceptic is anything but a disreputable quitter? How could we be persuaded otherwise? And it would seem that, on the best scenario, a Sceptic convinced by argument that argument gets you nowhere should consistently abandon philosophy; and how could that be a tenable *philosophical* position?

The ancient Sceptics had answers to such questions, answers of a type to contribute directly to our main topics. First, take (in)consistency and self-refutation. To count as philosophical, a Sceptic must discredit a doctrine by eroding its rational underpinnings. The Sceptic claims the ability to do so globally. The danger of inconsistency immediately rears its head: for if global Sceptics deny quite generally that argument is effective, how can they put it to work? And when they claim that there is no exit from *aporia*, is that claim an *assertion*, viz commitment to a truth? In which case, are they not clear about the universality of *aporia*, and so not exceptionlessly puzzled? However that might be, what will remain to them, in the way of commitments for getting on with? Consider an extreme example, schematically expressed. A Sceptic declares to you: 'nothing can be known'. You listen patiently and attentively to their case. At the end you reply: 'you certainly did expound an argument, defining what you meant by "knowledge", and arguing that it is unobtainable. I needn't go into details, since you are behaving in a ludicrous manner. For suppose your argument is a proof. In which case we would *know* to be true its conclusion – that we can know *nothing* to be true. Which is silly as can be. So your argument is no proof. In which case, why need we accept its conclusion? We cannot *know* that nothing can be known! Of course, that something is not or cannot be known might be true; but your grand proposition, if true, is strictly unknowable. Either which way, you cannot consistently argue for it, so you have no claims on philosophical attention; and if your reaction is to believe it but give up any pretension to arguing in its favour, you have achieved consistency, but only at the cost of abandoning the practice of philosophy altogether. So if your ilk are not inevitably defeated, the best you can hope for is a Pyrrhic victory'.

The more ambitious the scope of Scepticism, the more vulnerable it proves to dialectical attacks which often turn on charges of self-refutation. Is any defence forthcoming? It begins with etymology. 'Sceptic' derives from the Greek word *skeptesthai*, which means 'to examine or investigate'. If we are having a philosophical discussion, I might present a so-called *ad hominem* objection to your views. 'You are committed to the truth of *X*. Do you accept *Y*? Yes. Well look, here is an argument which starts from *Y* – do you accept that it is a sound argument? Yes. But see, that argument concludes that *X* is false. Your beliefs are inconsistent, and you had better adjust your commitments.' Notice that I might myself believe in *Y*, and the validity of the argumentative challenge; but then again I might either not have this belief, or even believe that *Y* is false, or the argument invalid. That is irrelevant; the important thing is your commitments, to both the truth of propositions and the validity of arguments, and how I might exploit them. In many Platonic dialogues, including the *Theaetetus*, Socrates is represented as claiming not to know the answers to the questions which he poses. When his interlocutors adopt positions, he proceeds to test them through *ad hominem* argument. In the Hellenistic period, the Academy, Plato's school, became a centre of scepticism. For the Hellenistic Academics, the aporetic Socrates exemplified the right way to do philosophy; they engaged in debate with their competitors, drawing on an armoury of dialectical tactics and strategies designed offensively to refute the opposition by their own lights, and defensively to rebut accusations of inconsistency and self-refutation. Seeing that uncommitted examination may be a viable philosophical option will enrich our appreciation of Greek methods: the worth and interest of dialectic can lie in method, rather than substantive results.

These Hellenistic followers of (a version of) Socrates are not the philosophers known to history as capital-S 'Sceptics'; that title properly belongs to another movement, claiming as its figurehead a certain Pyrrho, born several decades after Socrates' death. These Pyrrhonists or Sceptics are remarkable for their self-conscious reflection on how to keep on examining without falling prey to inconsistency. But what is especially noteworthy for us is that Scepticism amounted to more than a kit of dialectical techniques: its adherents talk of it as 'a way of life'.

This is important to us for two reasons. It is a sad irony that we speak of a '(merely) academic' question when we mean that its resolution has little or no bearing on what really matters (for most people, university philosophy is the star example of the 'merely academic'). This is ironic because the ancient Academics regarded their pursuits as anything but trivial. In general, ancient philosophers conceived of philosophy not as a narrow profession or avocation, but rather as a whole way of life – in fact the best sort of life, since the best or only chance of achieving human excellence was seen as residing in successfully living the philosophical life.[12] That is our last theme. What does it mean to do philosophy in a way which amounts to living the philosophical life? How could involvement in dialectic be so great that one's essential identity is 'philosopher'? The second reason we shall explore philosophy as a way of life has to do with Scepticism in particular. Sceptics claim to live the 'life without belief': what could that mean, and how could it be possible? If I believe nothing, how could I react to any stimuli, how could I survive, let alone carry on reasonably? Why not exit by the window rather than the door, if I don't believe it makes any difference? If I don't believe there is a cliff in front of me, why not plummet over? There was a dispute about whether Pyrrho needed 'minders' to escape such a sad fate; it will show us more about how philosophy takes shape by fixing on one or another history. And you might wonder: even if a Sceptic might survive, wouldn't that be a grim life, having relinquished any prospect of knowledge? How could a permanent state of *aporia* be anything but a torment to be borne, to someone of a philosophical cast of mind? The Sceptics' astonishing claim is that the life without belief is the supremely fulfilled life; and they were, of course, careful not to put that forward dogmatically.

Even within my self-imposed limits, I might have attempted to reach similar goals by different routes. For example, we might have stepped backwards in Greek philosophical history to include a life of committed belief – with a vengeance. In the *Nicomachean Ethics*, Aristotle argues that all human beings seek *eudaimonia*, which is something like happiness or success or flourishing throughout one's entire life.[13] How might one achieve success? You might imagine that there is no single answer to that question: if happiness is a place-holder for one's goal in life, different people will entertain different ambitions, and the means whereby they might flourish will differ accordingly. Aristotle will have none of that: just as it is true that this is a healthy dog, that a sickly one, or this a well-designed bicycle, that a useless one, so too there is an objectively correct description of an excellent human being, satisfaction of which yields the good life. His grounds for this conviction are an argument which ascribes a function to human beings. In general, if things of kind X have a function to perform, then there are impartial criteria for assessing whether and to what extent they succeed in discharging it. So were it the case that human nature is functional, philosophers might attempt to devise a true theory dictating how we ought to behave; if the details of the theory are sufficiently specific, relativists about ethical values will be left with no room to manoeuvre. In assembling his thoughts on *eudaimonia* Aristotle characteristically draws on the findings of conceptual analysis and the upshot of dialectical interaction with other philosophers and his larger cultural environment. So you might move on from this book to your own case study of Aristotelian philosophy in action, a philosophy which proposes a mode of living grounded in endorsed argument and substantive belief; and then set that beside the dialectical detachment and freedom from belief advocated by the Sceptics.[14] Or it would have been possible to convey how the tradition comes into being through discovery and invention of its own history by starting with Parmenides on what is not, and following through with Presocratic, Platonic and Aristotelian reactions to Parmenides' seminal argument. Again, another strand of the tradition is the debate over pleasure, what it is, and whether it should be indulged. Or, instead of the *Nicomachean Ethics*, you might turn to the Hellenistic schools for illustrations of moral theory which infers normative conclusions from purportedly objective views of human nature. But if this book succeeds in guiding you into the tradition of Greek philosophy, you will be free to explore independently all that, and much more.

Chapter 1

Opposition, relativism, contradiction

Heraclitus and Xenophanes are so-called 'Presocratic' philosophers, which simply means 'before Socrates'. Is this any more than a convenient chronological label? 'Hellenistic' is a temporal adjective marking out more or less the historical period in the Greek world running from the establishment of kingdoms by the successors of Alexander the Great to the eventual conquest of the Greek domains by Rome ('Hellenistic sculpture', 'Hellenistic literature', 'Hellenistic philosophy'); but 'Presocratic' claims to make a division that is intrinsic to philosophy, not borrowed from political periodisation. Why should one fix on Socrates as a boundary? And even if that choice is well-motivated, do those who come before him share anything in common beyond lacking whatever is reckoned uniquely Socratic?

The 'Presocratic' classification is anything but a modern invention; it originates with Plato and was made canonical by Aristotle. You may be familiar with A.N. Whitehead's motto that all philosophy is 'footnotes to Plato'. That is a large exaggeration – one might with equal (in)justice contend that all philosophy is commentary on Parmenides – but enshrines a major truth, that Plato more than anyone else fostered the idea of philosophy as an autonomous discipline.[1] Not all of this is done through Socrates – Platonic dialogues contain methodological prescriptions and exercises associated with other characters – but most is, and Plato made Socrates the most memorable and attractive figure in all philosophy. The composite portrait which the Socratic dialogues together paint incorporates several traits of the man Alcibiades in the *Symposium* insists is altogether unique. A partial catalogue: first, Socrates is in search of essential definitions, not what a word means, but what a thing is. Second, ethical items preponderate as *definienda*. Third, and relatedly, Socrates is an audacious rationalist, relentless in his faith that understanding how we should live will prove sufficient for our living the best life. Fourth, he pursues this all-important wisdom by engaging interlocutors in question-and-answer dialectic. Aristotle endorses this portrait. According to him, although earlier philosophers had made stabs at definition, none had approached the task with Socrates' care and concentration (not that Aristotle is not highly critical of both Socrates and Plato on definition). He confirms that the turn to ethics was a Socratic innovation; indeed, his usual name for the 'Presocratics' is *hoi physiologoi*, 'students of nature'. And although Aristotle has much to teach us about the techniques and arguments of Presocratic philosophers, he concurs with Plato in reserving definitional question-and-answer dialectic with its promise of personal salvation for Socrates.[2]

That Socrates inaugurated a momentous philosophical revolution is palpably true, indisputable because Plato's representation and Aristotle's support ensured that the Socratic watershed became a permanent feature of the philosophical landscape (if you wield sufficient authority as a philosophical historian, sometimes saying it is so makes it so). Therefore we can accept that 'Postsocratic' would be much more than a convenient chronological label;[3] but does anything positive bind the Presocratics together? Yes. Most of them, including Heraclitus and Xenophanes, did attempt to explain nature, *physis* (hence *physiologoi*) – although that interest will not be the focus of our concern. They emerge from the original matrix of rationalist speculation, and many Presocratics made contributions not only to what we consider 'proper' philosophy, but also to science (physics, astronomy, geology, meteorology, geography, biology . . .) and mathematics. Eventually, relatively distinct mathematical and medical traditions did appear, which sometimes evolved independently of philosophy, sometimes hybridised spectacularly with it. The Presocratics, sharing a formidable intellectual agenda, did react argumentatively to one another and to other claimants to wisdom. And if Plato's contribution to carving out a privileged niche for philosophy is second to none, he did not start from scratch: the Presocratics not only made themselves special; as the first philosophers, they were responsible for the initial, pioneering articulations of exclusivity. Heraclitus' movement to a place apart was decisive and extraordinary.

In the Introduction I adverted to the need for exegetical skills in dealing with the evidence; that need is especially pressing when we study the Presocratics, because our information about them is to be found in what is called 'doxography'. A 'doxographer' is someone who collects and records philosophical opinions. Doxography comes in all shapes, sizes and qualities. Sometimes we get what we can from a late antique digest yielding nuggets like 'Thales says everything is water'. Sometimes, if we're lucky, not just an opinion, but also the all-important argument supporting it is also preserved, at least partially (that the appended argument is close to the author's own reasoning can never be automatically assumed). Sometimes the compiler was a conscientious and intelligent researcher; and sometimes he was anything but, cobbling together his handbook from someone else's, not consulting the originals, and introducing all manner of distortions. And sometimes the doxographer is much more than that. For example, Sextus Empiricus, from whom we derive very many reports on both the Presocratics and the Hellenistic thinkers, is a Sceptical philosopher in his own right; and late Neoplatonic commentators like Simplicius are of cardinal importance –

although they are in the business of explicating Platonic and Aristotelian texts, they range broadly and deeply.

Now when we study Plato, we read an entire corpus of complete dialogues. When we study Aristotle, we read not finished treatises, but rather assorted teaching material, some in the form of elliptical and cryptic notes; but there's a great deal of it, all by Aristotle himself. However, when we study Presocratic (or Hellenistic) philosophy, we must get to grips with miscellaneous doxography, so, far from enjoying access to entire works, it is not unusual to have next to nothing of the original. Extensive portions of some writings have been recovered; but, in the vast majority of cases, the evidence is fragmentary, sometimes extremely so. It is usual to divide the surviving evidence into 'fragments' in the strict sense and '*testimonia*': a fragment is judged to be *verbatim* quotation, while a *testimonium* is indirect reportage (making the distinction calls for nice judgement, and often we cannot reach a unanimous verdict on the status of the data).

Let me describe the consequent challenges. First, it would be a grave error to imagine that once some modern scholar has culled the kernel of actual quotation or objective report from its surrounding doxographical context, you can afford to ignore that context. There are a number of reasons why this is a big mistake. As often as not, as I have said, the real status of the reportage is unclear; and sometimes, even when we're confident we have some of the actual words, where the quotation starts and stops might not be obvious. Second, many doxographers have their own agendas. For example, Sextus Empiricus is a Sceptic. This means that when Sextus cites someone approvingly, e.g. Heraclitus, that is because he is reading them as pro-sceptical, or at least proto-sceptical: by this point it will not surprise you to learn that Sceptics are in the business of forging their own version of the tradition. All quotation is selective. So, even on the best case scenario, when Sextus is quoting or reporting with scrupulous care, we might come away with the entirely misleading impression that that earlier philosopher really was some sort of Sceptic. Not at all necessarily so: perhaps other material, which Sextus conveniently omits, would create an altogether different impression. Third, all but the most lightweight doxographers organise their reports according to historical schemes, lineages or 'schools'. A, the founder, had these ideas; B, his student, developed their implications, or modified them somewhat; C, B's student, changed the doctrine in defensive reaction to criticisms from X, a member of a hostile school, or perhaps synthesised B's teaching with the ideas of M, from a distinct but complementary school. And so on and so forth, sometimes in very complicated patterns. Such patterns of organisation originate with Plato, whose dialogues make claims for various affiliations and conflicts between earlier thinkers. What is fairly unsystematic in Plato becomes elaborately systematic in Aristotle; and his students carried the project much further and produced studies which are the ancestors of much subsequent doxography. This in its turn, of course, requires nice judgement, as we ourselves participate in the creative maintenance of the Greek philosophical tradition.

The implication is that this material makes daunting calls on interpretation: is that really what Xenophanes said? Sort of what he said? Did he say it for the reason indicated, if any? Can we extrapolate from this fragment to what's missing? Now you might think that this is a massive advertisement for not doing ancient Greek philosophy, that I'm saying you must achieve mastery of the whole thing, strictly philosophical and more or less doxographical, in order to get any sort of handle on one or another Presocratic. Well, in a way I am saying that: if a terrifying prospect, it's also exhilarating, because ancient Greek philosophy really is unique in its sheer interconnectedness, a whole thought-world. But in another way I'm saying nothing of the kind, at least without heavy, and reassuring, qualification. By all means avail yourself of the collections and guidebooks, which have made selections for you, predetermining many of these thorny issues so you can get down to interpretation. So far from trying to repress what I'm talking about, both Kirk, Raven and Schofield 1983[4] for Presocratics (KRS) and Long and Sedley 1987 for the Hellenistic thinkers take great pains to make such issues as transparent as possible. If you persevere with Greek philosophy, you will gradually find the contexts and connections of the tradition more and more accessible, and most likely come to disagree with some of KRS and Long and Sedley (not to mention me).

Heraclitus made himself felt early on: KRS 192 relates that his writings were so influential that he attracted disciples named after him, a bunch of 'Heracliteans'. We can't be chronologically precise about this: Cratylus, who figures in the Platonic dialogue named after him, expresses Heraclitean ideas, and the doxography identifies him as a Heraclitean, but that may be nothing more than inference from the dialogue, rather than independent testimony (although Aristotle's reportage, to be discussed in the next chapter, is emphatically not inferred from the *Theaetetus*). But it's safe enough to assume that in the centuries following Heraclitus' death, disciples did arise, probably advocating some version of his identity theory ('flux': more on this below). So we do have evidence for a Heraclitean movement. We should not imagine that it was a formal institution of any sort; but it is one of the very first attested tendencies or groupings, a sign that philosophy was coming into its own as a tradition. Heraclitus, Parmenides and Protagoras are the three predecessors, apart from Socrates, to exert the greatest influence on Plato; Aristotle devotes much critical attention to Heraclitus; and the Stoics adopted and adapted some of his physical theories. Heraclitus matters in all sorts of ways.

'[Of this *logos* which is always] men prove to be uncomprehending, both before they have heard it and when once they have heard it. For although all things happen according to this *logos*, men are like people of no experience, even when they experience such words and deeds as I explain, when I distinguish each thing according to its nature and declare how it is; but the rest of men fail to notice what they do after they wake up just as they forget what they do when asleep' (KRS 194).[5]

KRS 194 is usually designated 'fragment 1' in the belief, which I share, that it preserves the first lines of Heraclitus' book. So we should examine it with care; it tells us how Heraclitus introduced himself to his original audience, and thus presents an all too rare opportunity to gain some idea of how a Presocratic tried to communicate his message. If this is the very beginning of the book, then Heraclitus deliberately composed it as he did in the knowledge that his readers initially would have to interpret it in its own terms. And you might not be favourably impressed. I left the first words unconstrued because I disagree with the KRS translation, 'of the *logos* which is as I describe it men always prove to be uncomprehending'. The problem is how to disambiguate 'always' in the Greek construction. There are two types of ambiguity. The first is lexical ambiguity; this arises when a single lexical item has two or more meanings. For example, the word 'bank' can refer to either the shore of a river or a secure place to deposit money. The second kind is syntactic ambiguity; this arises when two or more interpretations of the grammar of a phrase are possible, according to how one groups the words together: for example, 'polishing machines can be dangerous'. The present instance is one of syntactic ambiguity. 'Always' has a single, fixed meaning, but does it modify what precedes, 'of this *logos* which is', or what follows, 'men prove to be uncomprehending'? Either option is permissible on linguistic grounds, so which is the correct decision?

Ordinary discourse is rife with ambiguity, but this does not, by and large, hamper communication. Let us start with lexical ambiguity. Were I to say to you, 'I want that money in the bank', you might immediately infer that I want the cash to be deposited in a vault, not buried by a stream; it won't even occur to you to be puzzled about the lexical ambiguity of 'bank'. But that is not the end of the story, since that inference would be too hasty: for perhaps I want to take home all the cash that is presently in the vault. That is, the English phrase 'I want that X in the Y' itself requires disambiguation, because there are two possible interpretations of its grammar: either X is a simple direct object, 'I want that-money-in-the-bank' (in which case I am requesting that you fetch money already there); or the predicate 'in the Y' is to be attached to X, 'I want that money (to be) in the bank' (in which case I am requesting that the money be deposited).[6] Thus this statement is four-way ambiguous, since it exemplifies both lexical and syntactic ambiguity at once; not that this would necessarily create special difficulties, since you would dissolve the syntactic ambiguity either on the basis of antecedent background knowledge of the situation, or by explicitly asking me what was wanted. Another example of syntactic ambiguity: if I say 'the campers were threatened by marauding bears, and the hero came to their aid', you will plump for the syntax which takes the campers, not the bears, as the antecedent of 'their'; it's not heroic to help the bears eat the campers!

Ordinary folk, theoretical linguisticians and philosophers of language by and large share the presumption that ambiguity is a bad thing. You don't want to be in doubt over what I'm getting at; students of language assume that clarity is a virtue in all communication systems. This assumption is eminently reasonable: if communication is for the transmission of information, we don't want the message to go astray. Problems can set in at two points in the system. First, the input can be fine, but the system corrupts it in transmission. For example, if you speak clearly into a good mobile phone, but the signal is garbled and the object of your affections hears 'I loath you' when you said 'I love you', think about changing your phone company. Second, transmission might be fine, but the input can be open to various interpretations. You hear me saying loud and clear, 'Jack is fine but Jill is wretched – isn't that wonderful!'. Am I kindly enthusiastic about Jack's good fortune, or maliciously pleased about Jill's unhappiness?

But if eminently reasonable, we should not conclude that the assumption is universally valid. To be so, it would have to be the case that all messages can, in principle, be formulated with total clarity, and so should be. Some areas of discourse fit that bill. Warning signs should be simple and unambiguous; in a good system of mathematics or formal logic, each symbol must have a single, well-defined meaning, eliminating lexical ambiguity, and devices such as bracketing should eliminate syntactic ambiguity. But consider the eccentricity of this exchange: ' – I love that poem! – Why? – It's completely straightforward and unambiguous'. I've betrayed my bad taste: much good poetry is good because it's complex; it's complex because the diction and syntax are open to multiple interpretation; and that's a good thing because more than one thing is being said. Also, the poet may well have chosen to leave the semantics undetermined, because the relation between the different things being said is itself unresolved. And sometimes the obstacles to immediate or complete comprehension are themselves the point: we are invited to experience the challenging and rewarding stress and strain of communication; if you like, the medium is the message.

And how does this bear on the unpacking of Heraclitus' first fragment? Were the assumption that clarity is always a good thing and should always be striven after valid, then unless he was perverse or incompetent, he must have intended one and only one syntactical construction. So is he a shockingly bad writer? The clumsiness could not be more glaring than at the beginning, when any decent writer would take care to make the best possible first impression. Unfavourable judgement of Heraclitus as a communicator is ancient. He was tagged the 'riddler'; Aristotle, for one, is impatient with his obscurity. I don't agree. I believe the syntactic ambiguity is quite deliberate on Heraclitus' part: he put it just this way because he wanted you to be uncertain of whether he is saying 'men *always* prove to be uncomprehending of this *logos*', or 'of this *logos* which *always* is, men prove to be uncomprehending'. And why wouldn't that be a perverse intention? Two possibilities, not necessarily exclusive: first, that Heraclitus' message has to be inherently ambiguous, because it concerns something inherently unclear; second, that ultimately a clear message will emerge, but it's good for us to have to work our way through to a clarity which we are not given on a plate, and have to earn. These possibilities must remain open until we really make progress with Heraclitus. So I'm suggesting that the correct way to construe the opening of the fragment is in unresolved triplicate: 'of this existent *logos* men *always* prove to be uncompre-hending'; 'of this *logos* which *always* is men prove to be uncomprehending'; and both ways at once, 'of this *logos* which *always* is, men *always* prove to be uncomprehending'. Don't disam-biguate – for now, at least.[7] And why have I left *logos* untrans-lated (as does KRS), however one reacts to the ambiguity? It is so important to Heraclitus that it would be fair to dub him 'the philosopher of the *logos*': since we do not (yet) know what his *logos* means, we should not pretend otherwise. This is our first lesson in careful philosophical reading (and an illustration of the importance of the skills of a classicist to those who do Greek philosophy).[8]

You might protest: 'suppose that for the nonce we accept your hypothesis that the ambiguity is deliberate, and is not to be immediately resolved. Doesn't that mean that Heraclitus was a dreadful philosopher? You yourself provided the example of a system of formal logic, which attempts to reduce ambiguity to the absolute minimum. Logic is used to represent the forms of arguments. If their premisses are ambiguous, then how can we tell whether the argument is valid? Taken one way, the inferences might be good; taken another, maybe not. So ambiguity might be fine in some poetical genres, but is to condemned as a bad defect in philosophy'. You should be worried on this score: both Plato and Aristotle warn us to be on our guard against those who exploit ambiguity to construct fallacies with which to fool us. To make matters worse: ' . . . men prove to be uncomprehending, both *before* they have heard it *and when once they have heard it*'. Isn't this Heraclitus shooting himself in his own foot? How can we be justly scolded for incomprehension before we have even been given the chance to understand? This seems to be a wilful paradox. And isn't it rebarbative to be told, apparently, that you anyway won't comprehend what you're about to hear? Or is it that we are implicitly invited – and challenged – to prove our-selves extraordinary people, much more intelligent than the com-mon herd? Time will tell whether Heraclitus can be acquitted of the charge of careless or even malicious exploitation of ambiguity and paradox-mongering. And it's not as if that's the only source of his notorious obscurity: he also goes in for puns and word-play, and expresses himself in a manner which – ambiguously – might be either literal or metaphorical. Difficult on purpose, but to what point?

And why is it that the ordinary run of people fail to compre-hend the *logos* (soon we shall think about what the *logos* might be; for now I want to leave it a cipher, to concentrate on issues of communication)? Heraclitus provides a cryptic answer: 'for although . . . ' indicates that the remainder of the fragment is a description of what usually goes wrong. First, the *logos* governs everything; second, Heraclitus claims to convey how this is so; but third, men are like inexperienced dreamers. Central to Heraclitus' diagnosis is the ironic contention that although the *logos* is omnipresent, and so must in some sense be very easy to apprehend – which might furnish a clue as to how we are rightly censured before we have heard it *from Heraclitus* – in another sense it eludes discovery, because of the human tendency towards solipsism. There is one real waking world, common to us all; but most people go on as if lost in dreams. Dreams are by definition unreal; and each fool inhabits a private dream world.

The need to embrace the universal is hammered home: 'there-fore it is necessary to follow what is common; but although the *logos* is common the many live as though they had a private understanding' (KRS 195). You might infer that no authentic understanding could be private or exclusive. But then what about: 'I searched out myself' (KRS 246)? How is it consistent for Heraclitus to demand allegiance to what is common, yet at the same time boast of his privileged wisdom?[9] Consistency is preserved if the idea is that while we do all inhabit the one real, shared world, most of us have our eyes clapped shut, as it were – were we like Heraclitus, we could open them and see the truth. You might complain that that reading goes against the grain of 'I searched out *myself*': that sounds like reflexive meditation aimed inwards, not gazing outwards. But we shall learn later that, on Heraclitus' conception, the world consists of small structures which are homologous with cosmic structure: therefore the universal is at once hidden and apparent in particular details, including the individual human psyche. This is absolutely characteristic of Heraclitus: he takes certain oppositions – here, common vs private, Heraclitus vs the rest of us – sets them in more or less violent or disconcerting opposition, and then prods us to puzzle over whether the opposition is total and rigid. At this juncture this is a matter of exposition, of formal comment on the *logos*; later we shall discover that the pattern is also exemplified in the nature of things. So Heraclitus not only deliberately exploits ambiguity; he also deliberately constructs tricky paradoxes. Paradoxes are of utmost importance in philosophy, and Heraclitus was the first to realise this. Parallel to the choices in dealing with ambiguity, one reaction to paradox is to resolve it, to show how, despite the appearances, things aren't really strange in that way; but another reaction is to insist that the paradox is irreducible, and somehow to persuade us that its truth should not be incredible.

'Listening not to me but to the *logos* it is wise to agree that all things are one' (KRS 196). 'To agree' stands for *homologein*, an untranslatable pun: wisdom consists in accordance with the *logos*; and that is because that single and universal *logos* unifies everything. More emphatic paradox: how can I hear what Heraclitus is saying, if I don't listen to him? The implication is twofold: that although Heraclitus is its mouthpiece, the *logos* is everywhere accessible; and that you'd better not take Heraclitus' personal word for it. But how can all things be one? Isn't Heraclitus himself isolated from the benighted masses? Maybe hidden connections underlie superficial diversity, so that all things are indeed one.

But now we should return to fragment 1, to address the cardinal, postponed question: what *is* the *logos*? Heraclitus underlines its urgency by writing 'of *this logos*': *which logos*? Evidently, given what we've already learnt about Heraclitus, a complete and clear answer is not meant to be forthcoming right from the start. Let's begin with the semantics of the word. It's polysemic. By that I mean a term which possesses neither a single and simple signification, nor an ambiguous one which can be taken in different and unrelated ways: polysemic terms do have multiple meanings, but these meanings are related, sometimes in subtle semantic patterns. A polysemic term is resonant: it means more than one thing, and these things resonate harmoniously. *Logos* can mean: a phrase or sentence; a larger discourse consisting of sentences, of any genre; what is expressed in that discourse, e.g. the argument of a philosophical discussion; a mathematical ratio or proportion; most abstractly, any structural arrangement or pattern. One must avoid a bad mistake which crops up often: *logos* does not mean 'word' (the source of this error is the biblical 'in the beginning was the Word', where 'word' is indeed used for *logos*). The reason that's a bad mistake becomes clear if we reflect on how the various meanings are related. At the semantic heart of *logos* lies the verbal meaning, but one extends out to the other significations from the fact of verbal plurality. A jumble of words, a random list, does not a *logos* make; the words must be so combined as to constitute, at the minimum, a meaningful phrase. A simple sentence makes sense, and it makes sense because of the grammatical relations between its words. A speech or piece of writing makes sense because of the various meaningful relations, narrative, logical, whatever, which obtain between its constituent sentences – otherwise it doesn't hang together. If one considers those narrative and logical relations in abstraction from their verbal expression, one gets to *logos* as reason or rationale; and *logos* as ratio or proportion ties together two or more quantities. So, at the most abstract, a *logos* L is whatever principle of organisation imposes a structure on a set of elements a, b, c ... Thus a single word taken in isolation cannot be a *logos*, because there are no other verbal elements to which it is related.

All these semantic implications should be brought to bear on the interpretation of Heraclitus. First, if his discourse is a *logos*, there will be all sorts of connections between the various things he says, to which we should be attentive. And that is so: you begin to understand him by attending to the ways in which different fragments play off one other through verbal echoes, structural similarity, and so forth. And together they build up to a single, global *logos*. Second, if 'all things happen according to this *logos*', Heraclitus is saying that his verbal *logos* represents the order of things; if he 'distinguishes each thing according to its nature and declares how it is' and 'it is wise to agree that all things are one', then we should expect there to be a principle or set of principles instantiated universally, which give the world a coherent structure.[10] It is this above all which makes Heraclitus such an exciting and original philosopher. Earlier Presocratics had asserted that the world comes from, and perhaps is, some stuff or another. But although Heraclitus does speculate that the world is somehow constituted from fire, what matters crucially is not what the parts of the world are made of, but rather how those parts are arranged and interact. One of Heraclitus' most important legacies to philosophy is a recognition that understanding comes from detecting patterns and structure.

So much for now on Heraclitus' designedly baffling mode of communication, his way of getting and holding our philosophical attention by using language to tease and defer understanding, to plunge us into a state of thorough *aporia* – as we continue, we shall deepen our sense of how persistently he provokes us dialectically. To add substance to our initially abstract idea of the *logos*, we must consider Heraclitus' statements about opposites, what they are, how they are related, and what their (omni)presence might signify.

'Sea is the most pure and the most polluted water; for fishes it is drinkable and salutary, but for men it is undrinkable and deleterious' (KRS 199). You might say: 'so what? Never mind about the biological facts; let's suppose that the fish are drinking. Still, I'm a human being, not a fish; and people rank much higher in the scale of things than fish; so much higher that sea water is most polluted'. This dismissal might come to your lips all the more promptly because you probably don't spend much time on piscine attitudes, and, if they are brought to your attention, are not likely to take them seriously as a challenge to your own opinions.[11] But perhaps you won't have such a ready response if we switch to a human example. In one of his most celebrated anecdotes, the ancient historian Herodotus relates that a king questioned some foreign visitors to his court concerning their treatment of the dead. The Greeks replied that they piously consume the corpses of their dead parents on funeral pyres. And what would be the greatest impiety? To eat them. The Scythians replied that they piously ate the corpses. And what would be the greatest impiety? To burn them. These are, of course, flatly incompatible ways of disposing of the dead – who is right?

Let us describe such situations abstractly and schematically. There is a question, Q: it could concern a plain matter of fact, e.g. is the earth flat or round? Or a theoretical matter, e.g. is matter infinitely divisible? Or how to behave, e.g. how does one properly dispose of one's mother's corpse? And there is a range of answers to Q, a, b, c . . . A, b, c . . . are not complementary; they are incompatible. The proponents of a, b, c . . . might be individuals, groups of individuals or entire societies, living in the same or different historical periods. And, crucially, we are aware of no good or decisive reason to plump for any one of these alternatives, in preference to the incompatible alternatives. When things are one way or another, but you have no sufficient reason to believe they are this rather than that way, the rational thing to do is to suspend judgement. (Of course, sometimes the rational thing to do is to take a chance: if my enemies are in deadly pursuit and I'm at a crossroads, ignorant of which path leads to safety, I'll do better to run down one at random rather than wait for capture; but such urgent situations are not at issue.) This can be a passing state of affairs. Now you have no idea whether I'll buy some food or a CD; but then you ask me; I say 'some food'; you have no grounds to question my sincerity; and so you have the answer. But sometimes the state of uncertainty over who is right is long-lasting, or even permanent. The Greeks and the Scythians stick to their guns; neither the Pope nor feminists give way over abortion.

What then is the rational reaction? There are two possibilities. Q has a true answer, but it is inaccessible to us. That might be for trivial or profound reasons. No one now knows what my mother had for breakfast on 2 February 1962; and no one will ever know. The fact of the matter is irrecoverable. But there is a fact of the matter which could easily have been ascertained, had anyone been interested in this trivia. There are certain mathematical problems which remain unsolved. Perhaps some future mathematical genius will crack them; but maybe no human being ever will, not because they are in principle insoluble, but rather because their solution requires a greater than human intelligence (don't be confident there are no such problems, in mathematics and elsewhere). Second possibility: the dispute over *a*, *b*, *c* . . . is perennial because nothing in the way things are, no matter how hard we looked, no matter how intelligent and honest we were, would settle *Q* one way or another. Again, this might be trivial or profound. I adore chopped liver, it makes you gag – what's the right answer to the *Q* 'does chopped liver taste good'? There is none: *de gustibus non disputandum*. No one could care less. Now let's consider the *Q* 'is it polite to eat with one's hands'? Around here, we answer 'no'; elsewhere, they say 'yes'. But it would be incorrect to say there's no fact of the matter, or that it's entirely trivial. It is true that it is polite in England to wield a knife and fork, and true in southern India that it is not. And you should not offend your London hostess by grabbing food off her dinner service.

Finally, what about the *Q* 'how does one properly dispose of one's mother's corpse'? You might go in for burial; someone else might have her body cremated. Is it a *de gustibus* situation? If you believe that when you're dead, you're dead, and your family and friends are a secular and relaxed bunch, that might be your inclination. Or could it be more like table manners? Perhaps someone from your background goes in for the full panoply of coffin and casket, while acknowledging, without judgement or condemnation, that different folk follow different funerary customs. But maybe you're a pious Jew, confident that God decrees that the dead must be buried in a prescribed manner, and insistent that cremation offends Him. Of course bad Jews, followers of other religions and atheists burn corpses, but it is true that they offend the one true God and are sinners. They can't be won round; so much the worse for them. Your secular sister feels otherwise, and condemns you as parochial, bigoted and deluded.

Heraclitus contends that if we listen to the *logos*, we shall come to learn that all things are one; and our agreement – if we become Heracliteans – will flow from the realisation that phenomena of opposition fall within unifying structures. Our assessment of this doctrine has begun with evaluation of the seawater fragment; and what we now find is that doing that obliges us to weave relativism into the discussion. How so? A common response to conflicts over the *Q*'s is to abandon the quest for resolution: 'it's (all) relative'. But, as philosophers, we must take pains to construct and analyse versions of relativism capable of withstanding serious scrutiny, whether or not they prove ultimately viable. A first step in this direction is to avoid vulgar, would-be liberal relativism. 'Of course, *we* believe that men and women should be treated equally, but some Afghanis don't think so. So it's true for us that equal treatment is correct, true for them that it isn't.' Stuff and nonsense – unless the relativist goes on to explain the meaning of 'true for . . . '. '*We* believe that the earth is round, but some ancient Greeks thought it was flat – and that was true for them.' If that is all the relativist has to say, we reply: 'no it wasn't. It's true, full stop, that the earth is round. Of course some ancient Greeks sincerely believed otherwise. But belief, no matter how sincere, how passionate, how obstinate, doesn't make for truth. It is a logical howler to suppose that anybody, anywhere, any time, can know anything but a truth: that follows from the very definition of "knowledge"'.

Relativistic reactions are not in order when sorting out *a*, *b*, *c* . . . can proceed rationally and fairly. If the champion of *a* is a blithering idiot, then *a* is plain false – for everybody, including its backer. If *a* is false, but *Q* is jolly difficult, then its champion is not an idiot. The earth doesn't look round, so before various astronomical discoveries and theories, the circumnavigation of the globe, etc., one might be excused for being a flat-earther.

That doesn't mean that the flat-earther is, or ever was, correct. You might be feeling restive about my assimilating the treatment of women to the shape of the earth: perhaps you regard the issue of women's rights as a Q ripe for relativistic treatment. Fine: it is characteristic of relativism that whether certain Q's fall within its scope is itself open to dispute.

To complete our abstract schema. Suppose we agree that Q requires a relativistic response; there are still choices as to how we regard the competing and incompatible responses $a, b, c \ldots$ These choices arise from our attitude to the concept of truth, and open the way to a sophisticated formulation of relativism. 'Relativism' is so-called because the $a, b, c \ldots$'s are favoured relative to one or another point of view: it all depends on the perspective one adopts. So one might aver, as we did in seeing off vulgar relativism, that truth is absolute, not relative, not perspectival. If some Q's should be treated relativistically, that's because there simply is no truth of the matter: chopped liver tastes neither good nor bad, full stop; cremation is neither right nor wrong, full stop. This is fully compatible with its being true that I like it, and favour cremation: these are absolute facts about my taste and perspective. But one might react in another, quite distinct and radical manner: it's not that it's true that I favour cremation; rather, it's true-for-me that cremation is correct. Why the hyphens? To indicate that we are not just saying of some Q that it's relative; rather, we are asserting that truth itself is relative and perspectival. Whether this is a coherent assertion is much disputed by philosophers; in this chapter and the next we shall bring in Protagorean relativism, and Plato's and Aristotle's blistering attacks on relativistic theories of truth. Is truth absolute or relativised? And how many Q's are there? Note that these are not the same questions: one might believe that all truths are absolute, and that the Q's are few and far between; or that truth is absolute, but that the Q's are many, and very important.

At this juncture we step away from Heraclitus on opposites, since inspection of the doctrines of Xenophanes and Protagoras will help us with the issues of opposites and relativism.[12]

Xenophanes is the founder of 'rational theology', that is, of the investigation of divinity from an argumentative basis. This theology not only recommends a revolutionary theory of god, but also has far-reaching ethical implications: if god is profoundly different from what is traditionally imagined, it's not just our theoretical commitments which must be changed. God is worshipped, because it is supposed that it is right to do so, and that the divine assesses and reacts to human behaviour. Philosophical theology might suggest that there is a god to be worshipped, but that its attitude towards us is not what we think, so that the appropriate form of religious practice is not the traditional one; or that god is to be worshipped, although the divine doesn't mete out rewards or punishments; or, most radically of all, that god is to be studied, but that religion on the traditional conception is to be abandoned altogether, replaced by philosophical contemplation. It is often claimed that Greek religion is not doxastic: that is, that unlike Judaism and all the faiths descended from it, it was a matter of what the Greeks did in cults and festivals, sacrifice and ceremony, not of what they believed. There is truth in this: in the absence of an official creed, a holy text of unique status, you can be neither orthodox nor heterodox, because no *doxa* in particular is compulsory. There were plenty of stories about Zeus, say, and no one version was authoritative. This couldn't have meant that anything went: obviously an ancient Greek who insisted that Poseidon was more powerful than Zeus, the king of the gods, would at the very least raise eyebrows, and it is likely that his neighbours would expect him to come to grief. But this eccentric would likely not be hauled into an ecclesiastical court on a charge of impiety,[13] unless the community supposed that they would be caught up in whatever punishment Zeus might mete out. However, this characterisation shouldn't be exaggerated: action does spring from belief and consequent desire. (Why did I purchase some clothing? I believe that wearing this jacket will make me look good; I want to look good; so I buy it.) There might have been plenty of latitude over why the gods demand sacrifice, and over when to sacrifice, and over which animals to slaughter ritually; but a conventional Greek believed that they do so demand, and will be enraged if shown disrespect; and desired to avoid divine wrath; and so performed animal sacrifice. Wheel in a radical theological alternative, and all of that might well have to go. As we shall see, Xenophanes' theology was indeed a challenge – and a threat. The theology comes in two bits: a negative critique of various aspects of conventional religion, and then a novel positive theology, to replace what Xenophanes urges us to reject. We shall focus exclusively on the negative critique, which ties in with our running themes.

'Homer and Hesiod have attributed to the gods everything that is a shame and reproach among men, stealing and committing adultery and deceiving each other' (KRS 166). This is manifestly true. In Homer, Hermes steals the cattle of Apollo (although they later make friends); Zeus is, as it were, the patron saint of adultery; the *Iliad* has many incidents in which pro-Greek and pro-Trojan Olympians hoodwink one another. Examples from Hesiod include Prometheus' actually helping human beings to deceive the other gods by getting them to accept sacrificial portions which look good, but are inferior to what they retain for themselves; and he steals fire on their behalf. So the implication is that only beings who satisfy our moral standards are worthy of respect; the traditional gods do not satisfy those standards; therefore they are not worthy of our respect, perhaps with the further implication that, if not worthy of respect, they are *a fortiori* not worthy of worship.

It is possible to go further, by doing some Greek philosophy: let us imagine some dialectic on this topic. A defender of tradition might make several objections. First, he might contend that at least a considerable number of the examples don't hold water. Some of them, like that of Prometheus, concern dissension between members of the Olympian pantheon and other gods, in this case a Titan: Titans are indeed divine, but not first-class, ruling gods. Others, like some but not all of Zeus' seductions and rapes, involve the gods' behaving in what we regard as an immoral manner not towards one another, but rather towards human beings. So he might argue that *the* gods are the Olympians, and that relatively little of the 'in-house' behaviour, as it were, which the epic poets attribute to them is unethical. As textual evidence,[14] he might cite the strong association in both Homer and Hesiod of Zeus with justice: Olympian rule is precisely the justice of Zeus, the prevailing world order. And then he might attempt to defuse the remaining examples by pointing out that our human moral code – that is, the ancient Greek code – is not universal. If we are both Athenian citizens, and I either steal your cattle or rape your wife, I'm wicked and in big trouble. But if I do the same to a Spartan, let alone a barbarian, that's just life: if I'm still in big trouble, that's because they'll retaliate, not because I've done anything *per se* wrong – moral obligations have their limits, defined by the group to which one belongs. Second, he might adopt a concessive strategy targeted on the possible further implication that we shouldn't worship beings unworthy of moral respect. He concedes that there is indeed abundant evidence that the gods are amoral or even immoral. But he says that that has nothing to do with the relations we ought to maintain with them. Just as a human tyrant might be an evil monster, but demands and gets the servile obedience of his terrified subjects, so too we ought *a fortiori* to worship the gods – they are ever so much more powerful than even an Asian despot, a Greek byword for potent intimidation, so only an idiot would incur their wrath.

How might Xenophanes respond? First, he might attack the strategy of restricting moral demands to the internal relations of the Olympian pantheon in a number of ways. Hermes the thief steals the property of his fellow Olympian; and the most famous case of adultery in Greek literature is that of Ares having it off with Aphrodite, to the humiliation of the cuckolded Hephaestus. That is enough to show that *the* gods do wrong to one another, not just to outsiders. And he could press harder. It is indeed true that both Homer and Hesiod describe and invoke the justice of Zeus, but they do so precisely to emphasise its unrestricted sway.

Zeus is supposed to be the great upholder of morality throughout the entire world, not just at home on Mount Olympus. For
example, Hesiod ringingly proclaims that Zeus rewards good
kings who rule properly, but strikes down bad kings who exploit
their subjects: which is to say that he is the guarantor of justice,
as *we* understand it. So how could it be consistent for him to tol-
erate, let alone engage in, injustice? And as for the 'anything
goes, if you can get away with it' licence when one is dealing with
outsiders: that doesn't square entirely with traditional attitudes.
Two of Zeus' most important titles are *Horkios* and *Xenios*, the
god whose concern is with the oaths and mutual obligations
which bind together members of *distinct* societies: he is supposed
to punish those who break treaties or betray their *xenoi* (a *xenos*
is a 'guest-friend', a foreign individual or state to whom one is
bound by the sacred ties of hospitality). True, such relations of
mutual obligation will not automatically extend to all
barbarians – although it will to some, who might become *xenoi* –
but Olympian rule is depicted as embracing a great many human
societies within a single moral order. Thus once more the notion
that Zeus might legitimately play fast and loose with outsiders is
flatly inconsistent with traditional theology's insistence that he
embodies cosmic justice.

Second, we need not assume that the list of culpable divine
behaviour in KRS 166 is exhaustive. Let's recur to that famous
episode of Olympian adultery. Hephaestus cottons on and, in
one of Homer's best scenes, sets a successful trap, catching his
wife and her lover *in flagrante delicto*; the other gods roar with
laughter. And Aphrodite is mocked for her lack of prowess on
the Trojan battlefield, when she runs off after being wounded.
And Hephaestus' crippled hobbling routinely raises a laugh
amongst the other Olympians. So *the* gods regularly find each
other ridiculous, they mock one another. Again, Zeus is often
blinded by lust, and Hera takes advantage of this to distract him
sexually on Mount Ida. Again, for long periods – for instance,
during the prelude of the Trojan war, its duration and
aftermath – these gods are in violent dissension: Hera, Athena

and Aphrodite vie bitterly over the golden apple beauty prize; they battle against one other; Poseidon is Odysseus' nemesis, Athena, his protectress, who admiringly connives in his shifty tricks. Thus, in addition to theft, adultery and deceit, we might add unseemly amusement, lack of proper respect, and excessive passion and violence to the list.

Now suppose that the defender of the tradition attempts to beat a retreat by engaging in some editing. He wants to hang on to the impressive bits – especially the justice of Zeus – and so decides to ditch the embarrassing episodes as false. There are non-philosophical instances of this strategy. For example, the poet Pindar famously insists that stories which attribute impropriety or worse to the gods are impious, untrue blasphemy. But this won't work. The problem is that there's just too much of it, inter-woven throughout the corpus of ancient Greek formal literature and informal religious narrative: once you start excising, you'll never stop. Furthermore, the lack of an official orthodoxy in ancient Greek religion to which I've alluded is a two-edged weapon. It can be wielded defensively: since Homer and Hesiod are not canonical texts, like the Bible,[15] one need not either endorse, explain, or explain away their every statement. But this can also be turned against the traditionalist: why preserve this rather than that part of the tradition? To avoid a charge of being arbitrary, one would have to articulate a set of theologically jus-tified principles and then apply them rigorously across the board. In other words, one would have to move from conventional reli-gion to rational theology in Xenophanes' company, and revamp the tradition out of all recognition.

It is worth dwelling on the admission that there is strife on Olympus – an admission which cannot be plausibly retracted. KRS 166 makes it clear that Xenophanes hammered this point home: the gods behave in ways we condemn to '*each other*'; and this particular criticism was to enjoy a vigorous afterlife, thanks to Plato. In the *Euthyphro* Socrates' hapless interlocutor sug-gests that one might define piety as acting in accordance with the wishes of the gods. Socrates embarrasses him by citing just the evidence we have been examining: piety cannot be what Euthyphro says, because to please one god is to displease another. The objection is lethal and does much to undermine conventional religion. In the second book of the *Republic*, Socrates pretends to clean up Greek literature, starting with Homer: every single passage which represents the gods as anything less than perfectly ethical is to be excised. But the exercise is probably intended as a *reductio*: a pitiful and vapid remnant of Homer would survive. Plato grasped the explosive implications of Xenophanes' critique, and transmitted their force to posterity.

Xenophanes' second possible response to the traditionalist targets the concessive strategy of admitting that the gods are an unsavoury lot by our standards, but nevertheless insisting that we should worship them out of fear of divine punishment. First, is it adequate to the religious facts? Only to some of them. It is true that much cultic practice on both the private and civic scales was apotropaic, intended to ward off misfortune and disaster which might well otherwise descend on us from the gods. But much wasn't. Sometimes the Greeks prayed to get good things, not merely to avoid bad ones. That is consistent with this traditionalist defensive strategy: this behaviour would be an analogue of currying favour with an immoral but dangerous human tyrant. However, they also sometimes just celebrated the gods; and they did so on the ground that the gods are sublime and magnificent, and so worthy of pious respect. And that again is flatly inconsistent with characterising them as ridiculous, and so forth. Xenophanes' attack on the immorality of the traditional gods was not only vastly influential within Greek philosophy; it also had a huge impact on pagan vs Christian disputes. Numerous Christian apologists – for example, St Augustine – would repeat his criticisms so as to dismiss Greek pagan religion as wicked through and through. Greek pagan philosophers did fight back. But they did so on behalf of a rational theology, the descendant of Xenophanes' constructive suggestions, and conceded the vulnerability of the non-philosophical tradition. Sometimes they did defend the Olympian pantheon or Homer, but they did so by interpreting the tradition in symbolic or allegorical terms to make it consistent with their philosophical religion.

The first part of Xenophanes' negative critique attacked the immorality of the traditional gods. If my evaluation was correct, it hits home: the tradition is riddled with inconsistency, and attempts to make it consistent fail. One cannot eliminate the bad bits, because there'd be no stopping; one cannot protest that the gods are moral, only not by our standards, since their implication in maintaining our standards cannot be squared with flouting them. The second part of the negative critique is even more radical. For one might have imagined that even if Greek traditional theology as such cannot be salvaged, other species of similar religion might be safe. That is, like very many other ancient and modern peoples, the Greeks thought of their gods as anthropomorphic. They are not like us, in that they are immortal, never get ill – although they can be injured – and are incomparably stronger and more beautiful than us. But they also are like us: Aphrodite is the sexiest thing around, but she's sexy in the way that Helen of Troy is – only ever so much more so; Zeus can strike you down with lightning, but that's only an ever so much more efficacious weapon than a spear, not something altogether different. In the strict sense of the word, these gods are not 'incomparably' greater than us; they are just very, very much greater, as it were the rich and famous to the nth degree. How else could they copulate with us? And that's why one cannot wriggle out of the embarrassment that they are unethical. But one might imagine that other species of anthropomorphism could pass muster, if their gods are superhuman, but ethically impeccable. Isn't that possible in principle?

The second part of Xenophanes' critique closes off that escape route: 'But mortals consider that the gods are born, and that they have clothes and speech and bodies like their own' (KRS 167). So far this is just to articulate the presumption that the gods are anthropomorphic – why should that rock the traditionalist? Of course Hesiod's *Theogony* relates the birth of the gods; but they never die, and Zeus, unlike his predecessors, will never be toppled from power. However, it is not safe to assume that articulation makes no difference. Not just in the religious sphere, but throughout all of life people carry on in a more or less irreflective state. Sometimes they cannot be roused from their dogmatic slumbers: 'why behave this way? It's traditional, stupid! Stop bothering and play along or we'll get rid of you, you weird troublemaker'. But sometimes they can, whether partially or totally. The articulation need not be at all unfair: it might scrupulously, subtly, accurately and fully lay out people's unconscious presuppositions. That need not leave the status quo undisturbed. For example, if you are an impulsive and thoughtless individual, setting before your eyes a forceful but fair description of your behaviour may well get you to stop and think: 'wasn't I being inconsiderate?' That's personal reflection. But when what is articulated is, say, the presuppositions of our social structure, or the goals in life we conventionallly pursue, the analyst will most likely be a philosopher. Remember that I flagged up self-reflection as an essential characteristic of the philosophical enterprise. Sure the gods are born. But 'that they have clothes and speech and bodies *like their own*' – think about the implications of that: are you entirely comfortable with gods who are super-celebrities? See, you assume they are comparable to us; now confront a possibility you've never considered, simply because you don't reflect: what if the divine is *strictly* incomparable to us? In raising this possibility, Xenophanes qualifies as a philosopher of world historical importance.

'The Ethiopians say that their gods are snub-nosed and black, the Thracians that theirs have light blue eyes and red hair' (KRS 168). I do not know whether this is true, although it's likely enough (cf. e.g. some Mexican or African images of Christ, or Italian Madonnas). One presumes that Xenophanes and his contemporaries believed it, at any rate. What is the significance? One can run the implied argument in three versions. (1) We all say that we worship Zeus; but we endow him with our own physical characteristics. (2) We Greeks say that we worship Zeus; the

Ethiopians and the Thracians worship a supreme god, to whom they give different names, and whom again they endow with their distinctive physical characteristics. The truth is that it is one and the same god; and some or all of us acknowledge this identity. (3) We Greeks say that we worship Zeus; the Ethiopians and the Thracians worship a supreme god, to whom they give different names, and whom again they endow with their distinctive physical characteristics. We either deny that Zeus is identical to the Ethiopian or Thracian supreme deity, or aren't sure. There is documentary evidence that at least some of these possibilities actually obtained. For example, in Herodotus you will find both the claim that a Greek god is worshipped under the same or a different name elsewhere, and mention of exotic foreign deities unknown to the Greeks.

But on any of the three versions, it is easy enough to derive a conclusion which should disconcert the traditionalist. Zeus, no more than a human being, can have eyes which are both brown and blue (ignore the red herring that the gods can take on different appearances when in disguise; at issue is what they really and truly look like). If the gods are anthropomorphic, and human bodies come in distinct physiognomies, then Zeus looks like Zeus, and no one else. You might think that even if you haven't clapped eyes on someone, you might nevertheless have a general impression of their appearance. The gods are supposed to be bigger, stronger and better looking than anyone else (unless the god in question is the notoriously ugly Hephaestus, but never mind). So don't we know that Zeus is a bearded giant with piercing blue eyes? No. That is how he is conventionally represented around here; not so elsewhere. But surely we Greeks are superior in every respect to the barbarians? Our image must then be the correct one.

That is a smug, parochial and inadequate response. While it is true that the Greeks were notoriously chauvinistic – most people are – they also displayed a growing awareness of, and sensitivity to, racial and cultural diversity; Herodotus is the great treasure trove of relevant anthropological material. It is well known that sometimes Herodotus describes exotic barbarians in order to construct a picture of barbarism to be compared pejoratively with familiar Hellenism: we appreciate who 'we' are through contrasts with various inferior 'others'. But sometimes these exercises do not function straightforwardly to shore up pride in ethnic identity. For example, his treatment of Egypt is in part a textbook study in exotic inversion. Weaving is woman's work in Greece; in Egypt the men do it. Greek men piss standing up; Egyptian men crouch down, like Greek women. So far what is going on is denigration of effeminate Asiatics, or a fantasy to that effect. But Herodotus is also deeply impressed by the antiquity and perceived sophistication of the Egyptians, which he contrasts with Greece to the disadvantage of the latter. It is not the case that a thoughtful Greek would be unaware of alternatives, or immediately prefer homegrown to foreign beliefs and practices.

Note that this theological foray has brought us back to the vicinity of our point of departure. Men and fish are at odds over the quality of seawater; Greeks and Thracians are at odds over the physical appearance of the gods. Let us apply our abstract schema. Q is: what do the gods look like? To plump for either the Greek, or the Ethiopian, or the Thracian option, to the exclusion of the others, would be just plain silly and indefensible. Your reaction might be: we face a question which has a true answer, but an inaccessible one; there is an anthropomorphic Zeus, only we don't know what he looks like. Is that a comfortable position to occupy? Not altogether. Consider Christian images. A Raphael Madonna needn't at all resemble a Titian Madonna. Big deal, you might say: one of the purposes of such religious paintings is to evoke a pious reaction from the viewer. So what if the models were two different young women? So long as the viewer prays to Mary, the paintings are successful; since she was a young woman, and images can and do serve as focal points for meditation, that these are not likenesses of the real Mary is irrelevant. But if you're an orthodox Christian, then you are committed to the proposition that God became man at a certain time, in a certain place. Jesus of Nazareth was a certain height, his hair was one colour, not another – odds are he looked Jewish. And since he was, for you, the most important person who ever lived, his appearance is not neither here nor there: thus the controversy over the Turin shroud. Human beings communicate in important and intimate ways by looking at one another; in Heaven, you will see Christ's own face, and that will be a beatific vision. Back to the Greeks. If we haven't the foggiest idea of what Zeus really looks like, then he is much more remote from us than we had imagined. Of course the Olympians are remote: human beings do not penetrate their home on Olympus, and the divine is mysterious and awesome. But all anthropomorphic religions, among them ancient Greek polytheism and Christianity, presuppose that, in another sense, the divine is not remote: it wears a human face. Both the ancient Greeks and all Christian groups believe that their gods have not only walked among us – the select have also enjoyed revelation, they have recognised the physical presence of god. Xenophanes has poured scepticism over this faith.

But now go further. What if the correct response to 'what do the gods look like?' is not 'we can't be sure', but rather 'this is a relativistic Q'? The upshot would be either, if one goes in for relativised truth, that it is true-for-the-Thracians that he has red hair and blue eyes, true-for-the-Ethiopians that he has a snub nose and curly black hair. But a single individual can't be both at once; so there's a whole bunch of Zeuses. How could they *all* be the supreme deity? There's only *one* cosmos, isn't there? So Zeus does *not* rule OK. Or, if one goes in for absolute truth, the upshot would be that while it's true enough that Zeus is variously represented, there is *no* truth of the matter about his hair colour, etc. But were Zeus anthropomorphic, there would have to be: no one can have hair which isn't coloured. So Zeus *isn't* anthropomorphic. I've drawn this inference from KRS 168: it isn't there explicitly, and perhaps the traditionalist might resist it. But the next fragment is certainly intended to overcome such resistance: 'but if cattle and horses or lions had hands, or were able to draw with their hands and do the works that men can do, horses would draw the forms of the gods like horses, and cattle like cattle, and they would make their bodies such as they each had themselves' (KRS 169). This is the most famous remnant of Xenophanes – and deservedly so. I believe not only that KRS are correct to place it right after 168; I further speculate that this sequence preserves how Xenophanes originally unfolded his negative theology. His dialectical strategy is to soften you up by directing your attention to human diversity, so as to erode your confidence in your presumptions about the divine nature; and then to shake you up violently by going beyond humankind altogether (just as Heraclitus brings fish into the argument and, in other fragments, asses, pigs and chickens).[16] Xenophanes is not saying that cattle, horses and lions are religious, after their own kind; his assertion is a counterfactual. This is what philosophers call a 'thought experiment'; the fragment is our earliest attested example of a philosophical move whose importance cannot be exaggerated.

What is a thought experiment? An ordinary experiment is of the 'suck it and see' type: don't know whether you like oysters? Swallow one. Philosophers continue to disagree over what a scientific experiment is, or should be. That is because scientific experiments bear some relation to scientific theories, and since philosophers disagree over what such theories are, their relation to experiments remains unresolved. Let it suffice to say that they somehow testify for or against a theory; and they are so constructed as to bear on some aspect of its truth. Philosophers, who are armchair scientists, do not get into a laboratory and make something happen. In an ordinary experiment, we have no experience of X, but what X is is not in question (oysters are at issue, not chicken); so we have the experience, and judge the result. In a scientific experiment, the trick is to identify X; first we design a critical experiment, and then conduct it to produce an X which is, we hope, evidence for or against a theory. In a philosophical thought experiment, we don't *do* anything at all. Instead, we imagine that X obtains, and then assess the counterfactual implications for whatever is under investigation.

But just as good scientific experimenters follow proper methodology, so too good philosophical experimenters must construct and interpret their counterfactuals correctly. They are saying: 'were *P* the case, then *R* would follow; and that means . . . '. So we must ask three questions: is it acceptable to postulate *P*? That is: some *P*'s just happen to be false, and can become true: nothing's stopped you from scoffing an oyster, you just haven't yet. But the antecedents of philosophical thought experiments almost always are not only currently false; they usually could not be made true, to the best of our knowledge. For example, Aristotle thinks that the earth is at the centre of the cosmos, and asks us to imagine what would happen, were it displaced from that location: in the Aristotelian universe such dislocation is impossible. There are some impossibilities which aren't worth thinking about. That might be because they involve a contradiction, and so actually can't be thought about at all, e.g. round squares, or objects green and red all over. Or that might be because their obtaining would involve so many and such great changes of fact and law that the scenario is too remotely exotic to consider. Thus the first task is to decide whether to accept the invitation to imagine that *P*. If we do, the second job is to decide whether it is true that, if *P* obtained, *R* would follow: is this a valid counterfactual? The third job is to decide whether the experimenter is correct that such an implication really does have the claimed bearing on the way things actually are. You will understand that, in the nature of the case, there can be no set procedure for the performance of these jobs; a nice combination of conceptual analysis and speculation constrained by shared intuitions is called for.

So how does Xenophanes fare? His *P* is: animals have the intelligence, inclination and physical means to create their own gods. Let's cautiously think about that impossible state of affairs. Of course, what that involves is thinking about *us* endowed with a few non-human characteristics. (In Kipling's *Jungle Book*, the animals are really types of people who think and talk about what it would be like to live in a hierarchical pack, and so forth.) His *R* is:

then they would come up with gods which resembled themselves physically. Would that really follow? Here intuitions may well differ. Perhaps frogs would worship a divine snake: pray to great Snakey, and he might prevent his mortal progeny from swallowing you up. But maybe they would pray to the grand Batrachian. Why think that? Now we see why KRS 169 rightly follows 168: if different human races divinise after their own kind, let's make the inference that different animal species would follow suit.

And what bearing does Xenophanes claim this has on the way things actually are? Unfortunately, the fragment doesn't tell us; but I think we can work it out. The Thracian Zeus is a fine figure of a superman – by Thracian standards. Analogously, Zeus of the horses would be a magnificent piece of horseflesh – by equine standards. But Zeus could not be both a man and a horse! How does this take us beyond KRS 168? Xenophanes' culture assumes that the gods are greater than us, while we are greater than the other animals. Suppose that you're a racist Greek who considers Ethiopians physically inferior; then you imagine that Zeus resembles you more closely than he does an Ethiopian. But even an Ethiopian Zeus would be preferable to an equine god: Zeus could not look *worse* than any human being. Xenophanes agrees, of course. But the message of the thought experiment is that the divine is so superhuman that it is little more grotesque to contemplate animal gods than human ones. Compared to a frog, you're very fancy.[17] You agree that you're nothing fancy next to god, but are fatally mistaken in imagining that that's because his body is like yours, only ever so much better. Anthropomorphic gods are no more acceptable than non-human, zoomorphic ones. This concludes our investigation of Xenophanes' negative critique of conventional religion. He was no relativist or atheist; in his positive theology, he went on to introduce a monotheistic religion whose god is not anthropomorphic, and does not behave like the Olympians. But we have seen how he uses powerful types of argument some of which he shares with Heraclitus, and which might be deployed to very different effect by a relativist.

Now we turn to Protagoras, the arch-relativist of the Greek philosophical tradition. What sort of philosopher was he? So far from abjuring argument, he is said to have maintained that there is no issue concerning which one cannot construct a pair of opposing arguments. He engaged in linguistic analysis and advocated linguistic reform; wrote a thoroughly agnostic theological treatise; offered to impart skills which would bring success in politics; and engaged in high politics himself, writing the law code for a new Greek city. Did anything draw his philosophical activities together? Here we face a historical conundrum, for the tendency of the Greek philosophical tradition to create its own past is nowhere more apparent than in the case of Protagoras and his kind (if they were a well-formed kind). They were (usually older) contemporaries of Socrates; and, in dialogue after dialogue, Plato portrays these 'Sophists' unfavourably. He depicts them as a venal lot, peddling their dubious intellectual wares for considerable fees (Socrates charges nothing); puffed up with vain conceit (Socrates disavows knowledge); indeed arguing, sometimes with energy and facility, but all too often actuated by an unprincipled lust for dialectical victory (Socrates' goal is the truth, and nothing but the truth): thus 'sophisms'. The word 'Sophist' derives from *sophia*, wisdom; the scabrous Platonic characterisation of the Sophists insists that they are neither wise, nor seeking wisdom, and thus not genuine 'philosophers' at all ('philosopher' means 'one who loves wisdom'). This is the overwhelmingly negative part of the Platonic drive towards philosophical self-definition: Protagoras may have been the first and greatest Sophist, but that amounts to no more than his being cast as Socrates' most worthy foil in such dialogues as the *Protagoras* and the *Theaetetus*. This hatchet job (to which Aristotle in his turn contributed) proved so successful that it cannot now be undone: even scholars who indignantly reject the Platonic line as a pernicious fabrication have no choice but to view these 'victims' through a Platonic lens, since independent evidence is so exiguous (for Protagoras, we have only the opening sentences of his theological treatise and of a work named *Truth* or

Refutations, to which we shall come). Their most ardent defend-
ers speak of 'the Sophists', employing the Platonic term. In the
next chapter we shall do philosophy with the Protagoras of the
Platonic tradition; now we shall do the little we can with the pre-
Platonic figure.

What does seem to demonstrate that the Sophists deserve
recognition as a real movement, not defined polemically as un- or
anti-Socratic, is also what establishes their philosophical credentials: their enthusiasm for rhetoric, the study and use of communication for political ends, blossomed into theorising on the nature
and powers of *logos* itself. Why is Protagoras the supreme
Sophist? Here is the opening sentence of his *Truth*: 'man is the
measure of all things, of those that are that [or "how"] they are,
of those that are not that [or "how"] they are not' (fragment 1,
from Sextus Empiricus). What does this mean, and how did
Protagoras argue for it? Since that is the sum total of the surviving *Truth*, we cannot recover the arguments Protagoras adduced
in favour of his relativistic Measure doctrine; all we can do is pose
a few questions whose cautious answers should, in charity, be
compatible with what else we know of the historical Protagoras.

First, why is man cast in the role of measure? What about
Heraclitean fish? Maybe Protagoras meant 'as far as man is concerned . . . '; or maybe arguments for our supremacy as arbiters
of reality have vanished. Second, what is the scope of 'all
things'? Does it mean just what it says; or should it be so quali-
fied as to read 'all human affairs'? Third, and most important,
what is it to be a measure? Ordinary people take it for granted
that thinking or wishing that it is so doesn't make it so: Robert
Wardy's belief that this is a wonderful book doesn't generate literary success; only if the book is, as a matter of fact, wonderful
does my optimistic belief come out true, by virtue of correspondence to that fact. And philosophers have constructed theories
of objective truth which try to explain how our thoughts must
be related to the world so as to be true of the world. Some of
these theories incorporate the notion of correspondence, others
don't; but, if objectivist, they all alike assume that the direction

65

of fit is from world to thought, that our true beliefs must conform (if not 'correspond') to an independent reality. How could
Protagoras have imagined otherwise? For whatever reason,
either he must have supposed that the world comes to conform
to our beliefs, or perhaps he abandoned the notion of correspondence altogether, so that 'true' beliefs must be characterised
internally, as it were, in terms of some state of mind, without
reference to an external world. You might think that if 'all
things' means 'all things', and there is nothing external to which
our beliefs correspond, then anything goes, all beliefs are triv-
ially true. This cannot be what Protagoras intended, since he
offered to teach skills for changing other people's beliefs, and
thus must have supposed that a standard for the evaluation of
belief other than correspondence is available. Consider his interest in statecraft: maybe 'man' in 'man is the measure' should be
taken collectively. Imagine that all my readers agree that this is a
wonderful book – mightn't that make it so? An objectivist might
deny this – loads of trash is deplorably, if almost universally,
popular – but it is fairly easy to understand how, if the human
mind actually creates something, our attitudes towards it might
define its qualities – at least many of them. Would my fan club
make it 'true' that this book is wonderful? Suppose that the general view is that reading it is a profitable experience – profitable
because pleasant, thought-provoking, stimulating in all sorts of
ways . . . And that it continues to happen that new readers
regard themselves as better off for the experience. If the corporate judgement is and remains favourable, then the book is wonderful; if people throw it aside with disgust, the book is awful.
The criterion for 'truth' is what feels right; 'falsehoods' are to be
deprecated because commitment to them is disadvantageous,
again by a subjective standard.

What if I persist in a lonely conviction of my book's merits,
against society's verdict? If 'man' is to be taken collectively, then
I seem to entertain a false belief; if 'man' can have variable scope,
then it would seem that what is true for me is false for everyone
else. Well, if truth is a state of mind unanchored in independent

objects, then of course there is no difficulty in our attitudes diverging; and, if my current belief makes me indignant and wretched, perhaps I would be better off changing my mind, making it true for me too that this book is a turkey. Why does my translation have the variants 'that / how things are (not)'? The Greek can be translated either way, and much hinges on the difference. If one plumps for 'that', then Protagoras seems to be saying that we create the world; and if 'all things' is unqualified, not limited to cultural products, then if I think that the wind is cold and you don't, we are both right (this example is from the *Theaetetus*, but is probably Protagoras' own). But how then can we communicate? We naturally assume that when you say 'the wind is cold' and I say 'the wind is not cold', we are disagreeing because '*the* wind' refers to one and the same object. How could one and the same wind be both cold and not cold? If there is no independent wind out there to which only one of our beliefs could correspond, then we are not disagreeing; and you might be better off coming to share my perception (after all, it's more pleasant not to feel chilly). That would still leave how we manage to communicate at all a dark mystery: if there is nothing independent to latch onto, how is discourse possible, if interlocutors must *share* a topic? That is why one might prefer to plump for 'how'. At least on this option, things do exist independently of us, while the truth about them nevertheless consists in the attitudes we adopt towards them.

We haven't got very far with the historical Protagoras: did he mean 'that' or 'how'? If 'how', did he discern the danger of solipsism and try to fend it off by arguing that we do inhabit a common world of objects concerning which we are the criterion of truth construed as some type of successful attitude? Or did he focus on social utility, disregarding the logical and metaphysical implications of relativism? Our one sentence won't take us any further; it is the Platonic Protagoras who is obliged to field these questions, and his relation to the historical figure is enigmatic. But we have got somewhere. Heraclitus confronts us with (as yet unresolved and perhaps irresolvable) oppositions; Xenophanes insists that incompatible religious beliefs are suspect, and should be transcended; Protagoras, whatever the unfortunate gaps in our information, introduced to philosophy a relativistic strategy for dealing with (apparently) opposed beliefs, mediating between them through the adept modification of disadvantageous 'falsehood'.

Back to Heraclitus' seawater, with our question-schema ready for use: if species react incompatibly to it, then isn't it unjustifiably parochial to stick to our species' narrow perspective? One and the same water manifests properties not only distinct but opposed, depending on which sort of animal reacts to it: but how could water be like that? 'The path up and down is one and the same' (KRS 200). This fragment has been interpreted in sharply different ways. For some, it's about a common or garden path: Heraclitus is saying that, on an incline, whether the road is up or down depends on your starting- and end-points. For others, it's about the cyclical transformation of cosmic fire. Let us go for the first option. This reading doesn't rob the fragment of interest; if it relates a blindingly obvious fact, remember Heraclitus' warning that people blindly ignore what is there for all to see. You know very well that the path up is the path down; but have you stopped to reflect that it is one and the same? That is, first, that one and the same path manifests properties not only distinct but opposed, depending on where you're going; second, that although we've now had two examples of the possession of opposites, *how* they are manifested is not the same in the case of seawater and in the case of the path. 'Disease makes health pleasant and good, hunger satiety, weariness rest' (KRS 201). What is this saying? Not that disease *is* health, nor that one body exhibits both (although Heraclitus could have said that); rather, the moral is that we can only learn to recognise and appreciate certain conditions through experience of their opposite. 'For if it were not to Dionysus that they made the procession and sung the hymn to the shameful parts, the deed would be most shameless . . . ' (KRS 243). Some ancient Greek religious cults involved ritual worship of a sexual nature: perform the very same acts in one place at one time, and your behaviour is obscene; in another place at another time, your behaviour is pious (if the example seems *outré*, substitute what's fine to do in the privacy of your own bedroom, but not in the street – unless you're a Cynic). One and the same set of actions manifests opposed properties, depending on the context of performance. 'And as the same thing there exists in us living and dead and the waking and the sleeping and young and old; for these things having changed round are those, and those having changed round are these' (KRS 202). Now the opposites manifest themselves over time, through change: perhaps it is the soul which ages, wakes and sleeps – but what about the opposite direction? How does one get from death to life? Either souls are reincarnated, or new plants and animals are born from the remains of the dead. 'Things taken together are wholes and not wholes, something which is being brought together and brought apart, which is in tune and out of tune; out of all things there comes a unity, and out of a unity all things' (KRS 203). This is an abstract generalisation of the various types of unification of opposites we have surveyed, emphasising completion vs fragmentation, harmony vs disharmony, and that the patterns into which the opposites fall are dynamic, not static.

'They do not apprehend how being brought apart it is brought together with itself: there is a back-stretched connection,[18] as in the bow and the lyre' (KRS 209). 'They do not apprehend' is plausibly read as a deliberate reminiscence of fragment 1, where what is not apprehended is the *logos* itself; so this fragment is of considerable significance, since it perhaps reveals that the *logos* is a 'back-stretched connection'. And what could that mean? We have already learnt that some of the principles which structure things are in dynamic tension. You might object to Heraclitus: 'of course there are many kinetic phenomena; but it also looks to me as though much of the world is stable; and stable because it is static'. KRS 209 responds to this objection. Of course it *looks* that way; but: 'an unapparent connection is stronger than an apparent one' (KRS 207). The bow and the lyre appear to be static, harmonious structures. But the arms of the bow are actually pulling apart, kept arched by the tension of the string; to the observant eye, the apparent stability reveals a deeper instability. And the bow functions when the string is pulled, increasing tension: on release the arms are permitted to fly apart, until the string returns them to their original state. So it's not just that stability isn't static; were it not for dynamic opposition, there would be no unity. This is a beautiful example of Heraclitus' coherence in paradox, and an excellent illustration of his expository technique. He starts with a plurality of particular instances of opposition, leaving it to us to discern that and how the particulars manifest an unexpected unity. Then he abstracts to the universal, unifying *logos* present in them all; then he uses a simile to return to the particular, for the sake of vivid and memorable illustration. You may have noticed, however, that I have not cited KRS fragments in their order: who is to say that my suggested dialectical progress was Heraclitus' own? It is true that, apart from fragment 1, we don't know where the fragments came in his book; and my sequence is only one among many others – all equally speculative. But such reconstructive speculation is part of the fun of this aspect of doing Greek philosophy.

'It is necessary to know that war is common and right and justice is strife, and that all things happen by strife and necessity' (KRS 211). It follows from Heraclitus' espousal of dynamic tension that he paradoxically inverts the normal valuation of war and peace. War is common – that is, that is how the common *logos* makes itself felt. Now apply the recommended procedure for dealing with opposites. War and peace and justice and injustice seem to be opposed conditions; but since the more or less violent interaction of opposites yields patterns of shifting stability, they too are unified within the cosmos as a whole. There is likely to be pointed criticism of an illustrious predecessor implicit in this fragment. Anaximander, an earlier cosmologist, had declared that the world is (overall, in the long term) at peace, under the sway of restitutive justice; Heraclitus replies that that is so only if cosmic justice disconcertingly incorporates strife and conflict. He is not a comfortable philosopher.

To conclude our study of Heraclitus on opposites, let us address two questions. First, what is the extent of the doctrine? That is, he challenges us to pay heed to a *logos* which is at once his message, and a principle of cosmic organisation. This principle is evident in a whole range of oppositions which are variously united. But he declared that he reveals the nature of *each* thing, and that '*all* things are one': how does this book which you are reading manifest unified opposition as its essence? How do you? Two possibilities. First, that here we encounter an instance of Presocratic indulgence in bold or, if you like, foolhardy induction: Heraclitus crosses his fingers and just hopes that all things yield to his favoured analysis – somehow or other. But second, remember that 'unapparent connections' are stronger, and that 'nature is accustomed to hide itself' (KRS 208). The *logos* may be universal and set forth by Heraclitus: but it at once reveals and conceals itself. So encountering apparently recalcitrant cases is exactly what one ought to anticipate. A cynical response would be: how convenient for Heraclitus! But I think that would be unfair. Our survey demonstrated that he does not crudely insist that for any random *X* and *Y*, they are unified opposites, or possess properties unified in just the same way. Instead we saw that his examples are carefully selected to manifest unification in a host of interestingly *different* ways (my selection does not exhaust the variety). And note that in some cases, like the seawater, he holds your hand and specifies the respect in which the opposites become evident; in others, he leaves it to us to work it out. It follows that to claim that the *logos* is universal need not be mere bluff. Furthermore, we have seen that gaining awareness of the presence of opposites, and understanding how they are related, is a matter of enlarging our perspective: do not think in terms of the needs or interests of a single species; just because you prefer health over disease, do not neglect the fact that you can only come to appreciate one through the experience of the other. Because the *logos* is a *dynamic* cosmic principle, it might

71

well be there, but in shifting, large-scale, complex patterns to detect which would require heroic breadth and depth of perception. Ignorance is remaining within a partial, benighted perspective; wisdom comes the closer one approaches a holistic view. Heraclitus seems to claim that he has arrived there.

'God is day night, winter summer, war peace, satiety hunger; . . . he undergoes alteration in the way that fire, when it is mixed with spices, is named according to the scent of each of them' (KRS 204). The first part of the fragment, 'God is day night, winter summer, war peace, satiety hunger', seems to (try to) enunciate a contradiction, that there is a cosmic synthesis of what, on the small scale, cannot coexist. I can be hungry before lunch, sated after; but god is full and empty all at once. Were that so, then we cannot comprehend god or the world (which might be the same thing): the *logos* would be an ineffable contradiction. Contradiction is our final theme. Did Heraclitus' philosophy culminate in the unthinkable and unsayable? If so, is he not an anti-philosopher, a nihilistic mystic who obliterates the resources necessary to reason? So we broach our second question: is Heraclitus the fatally confused advocate of contradiction? In the middle of 204, where the dots come, there is the gloss 'all the opposites, this is the meaning'. Fragment 204 is from the doxographer Hippolytus, and KRS believe, and I agree, that it is a comment which has contaminated the quotation, rather than Heraclitus' own words. Nevertheless, the gloss is worth thinking about. You might read it as saying: for any predicate *P*, god – that is, the *logos* – *is* at once *P* and not *P*. But the second part of the fragment goes on: 'he undergoes alteration'. This no longer sounds like an attempt to enunciate a contradiction; if god changes, then he is no more full and empty all at once than you are. Or rather, given that the entire cosmos is so large and incorporates so many different things in opposed states, distinct aspects of it might well manifest every possible permutation and combination of oppositional relationship – which doesn't add up to a contradiction. Let us recur to the abstract generalisation of KRS 203: 'things taken together are wholes and not wholes, something which is being brought together and brought apart, which is in tune and out of tune; out of all things there comes a unity, and out of a unity all things'. This too could be read as contradictory, by latching onto 'wholes and not wholes', 'in tune and out of tune'; but 'being brought together and brought apart' and 'there comes' again indicate that change is going on.[19] Change dissolves the appearance of contradiction: I can't be sitting and standing simultaneously, but getting out of the chair removes me from one state and places me in its opposite. Does Heraclitus argue: 'fish live on seawater, but men die in it; therefore seawater is a contradictory fluid'? Not in KRS 199, he doesn't. Rather he first enunciates what sounds like a contradiction, and then resolves the paradox by adding the qualifiers 'for fish', 'for men'. Of course 'God is day night . . . ' *sounds* like a flat contradiction, but we have learnt that Heraclitus demands our getting beneath the surface of his words, and beneath the superficial appearance of things, to seek out the hidden and stronger connections.

This line of interpretation delivers a Heraclitus innocent of fallacious reasoning: for if he did conclude that seawater is a contradictory fluid – whatever that might mean – from its opposing effects on fish and men, then he was confused. (Just as if Protagoras did think that one and the same wind is cold and not cold, he too was confused: unless there is a common wind, but without intrinsic temperature, which is a relational property of the wind and its observers; or if all us solipsists have our own private winds – in which case Protagoras is a sort of inversion of a Heraclitus for whom contradiction is everywhere, since relativism would render it impossible. More on this in the next chapter.) If the sea is most pure for fish, it does not follow that it is most pure for men, too; but nor can one validly infer that it is most pure and most polluted, full stop – dropping the qualifiers is fallacious. In the Introduction I recommended sticking to a principle of charity in doing philosophy with the Greeks: attribute the best possible arguments to them, consistent with the evidence. In my view the direct evidence concerning Heraclitus on opposites is consistent with his not embracing contradiction; and, since arguments purporting to establish the existence of contradictions are fallacious, I am happy not to saddle Heraclitus with a theory which advocates the unthinkable. This version of Heraclitus deliberately sounds contradictory; but that is because his dialectic invites decoding, whereupon the paradox of contradiction is overcome. That I think the evidence is consistent with such a reading doesn't mean that it isn't false, because the evidence is incomplete and indeterminate. Alternatively, perhaps Heraclitus, clever as he was, descended into incoherence because philosophers had not yet thought hard enough about the nature of contradiction.

Plato in the *Republic* (436B) explicitly formulates the principle of contradiction – namely, that nothing can be at once P and not P, in the same respect, at the same time . . . : the appearances can seem contradictory, if one overlooks these various qualifications; but they are invariably specious. Maybe Heraclitus, in propounding his unification doctrine, was trying to say that things are at once P and not P, full stop; it took Plato to expose the futility of any such attempt. This version of Heraclitus, the Heraclitus of the tradition, is reserved for the next chapter. Not being a relat-ivist myself, I reject the idea that it's true-for-me that Heraclitus avoided contradiction, true-for-Plato-and-Aristotle that he sought to embrace it, true-for-you that . . . The real Heraclitus held to one, not necessarily fully worked-out, theory, to the exclusion of its incompatible alternatives. There is an absolute truth of the matter, but unless we recover more Heraclitus – and such amazing and delightful Presocratic discoveries have been made – that truth might remain forever inaccessible to us. The inaccessibility of truth is not a thing to be wished for, but it is not all doom and gloom. For even though the different versions of Heraclitus cannot coexist in reality, they remain good to think about and with.

Heraclitus is said to be the father of a doctrine of universal flux: what is it, and is there a connection with the unity of opposites? 'And some say not that some of the things which are are in a state of change, others not, but that all are always changing, but that this escapes our perception' (KRS 216). This report is from Aristotle; Platonic texts make clear that these people are Heracliteans: 'Heraclitus somewhere says that all things are in process and nothing stays still, and likening the things which are to the stream of a river, he says that you could not step twice into the same river' (KRS 215). This is from the dialogue the *Cratylus*; the interlocutor after whom it is named is a self-professed follower of Heraclitus. Cratylus was a real person, said by Aristotle to have been one of Plato's teachers; and the case for ascribing flux to Heraclitus would seem to be clinched by Cratylus' amendment of the doctrine: he 'criticised Heraclitus for saying that it is not possible to step into the same river twice; for he himself considered that it is not possible even once' (Aristotle, *Metaphysics Gamma* 1010a13 – 15). This doxography is completely unambiguous. According to it, Heraclitus believed that change is omnipresent; ordinary people assume that there are plenty of static and stable objects about, but in fact the entire world is in a state of perpetual flux. Why should Heraclitus have supposed that? We can reconstruct an argument on the basis of Aristotle's comment that 'this escapes our perception'. Perhaps Heraclitus observed that some things, like rivers, are ever-changing; others seem to change some of the time (e.g. when young you grew rapidly, but now you alter more slowly, and stay the same for long periods); others seem to be permanent (e.g. that mountain has towered over us from time immemorial). However, maybe this apparent fixity masks underlying fluidity. From day to day you look (more or less) the same; but, if we looked closer, we should see that our bodies are subject to myriad tiny changes, our minds are constantly restless (compare the modern belief that all the cells in your body are replaced in a short period). Nothing is as solid as rock; but, over the ages, even that mountain is slowly but surely eroded away.[20] Thus Heraclitus made a sweeping induction: everything always changes.

That is the traditional Heraclitus; flux is a captivating doctrine, and we have seen that an argument for it is forthcoming.

Furthermore, the notion that the world is paradoxically unstable, not what it seems on the surface, fits in nicely with 'nature is accustomed to hide itself'. But is it the historical Heraclitus? As with contradiction, so too with flux there are grounds for doubt, on two scores. First, at least in its extreme formulations, the theory has absurd and unacceptable consequences. Thought and speech require subjects; if we are thinking and speaking, there must be things we are thinking and speaking about. And these things must stay the same, for the duration: otherwise one objects, 'but you've changed the subject'. Now suppose that everything always changes, in every respect: then how could we manage to think or communicate, since by the time we made the utterance, the subject would no longer be as we said it was? Come to think of it, we would no longer be the same either . . . (There is an analogue with the difficulties for a Protagorean relativist in accounting for public discourse; this parallel will be discussed in the next chapter.) Of course, this sounds like a *prima facie* objection not to Heraclitus himself, but rather to Cratylus: if I can't step into the same river twice, I can manage the feat once, so short-lived objects survive for me to think and talk about.

But second, if the historical Heraclitus did advocate flux, he disappointingly misperceived the true implications of the phenomena which he observed. Take the river. If I argue, 'I cannot step into the Cam twice; for next time different water will be flowing over my feet', then I am sadly mistaken. That would be an acceptable argument, were the Cam identical with the water within its banks at any time; but it is not. The Cam is indeed a course of moving water; the water is its matter – were it to dry up, there would be no river – but it is also more than that, identified by source and outlet. There are simple stuffs – water, sand, mud – whose identity consists in nothing more than their material constitution. But more complicated objects are matter organised thus and so, and their identity depends on the maintenance of that organisation. So long as an animal's body continues to function, that its components are regularly replaced does not compromise its survival: the animal *is* the thing that functions, not the bits that perform together. The full development of this insight into identity is Aristotelian. Explaining identity in general and personal identity in particular is a long-standing philosophical enterprise, beset by many puzzles, and has occupied philosophers from antiquity to the present; I have only scratched the surface. But charity dictates that if the evidence permits us to ascribe a promising identity theory to Heraclitus, we should consider the possibility.

The Platonic and Aristotelian doxography does not; but other evidence does. 'Upon those that step into the same rivers different and different waters flow . . . They scatter and . . . gather . . . come together and flow away . . . approach and depart' (KRS 214). Nothing here about the rivers' disappearing: these are 'the *same* rivers'. What does Heraclitus seem to be saying, and why? Any ordinary fool can perceive the change – the water is not the same. But the river remains the same. How could that be? Change in some respect does not preclude lack of change in others; in fact, were the river to stop flowing, it would become a stagnant pond – so far from change being incompatible with identity, in this instance it positively demands it! Another advantage of this reading is that there is an immediate connection with the doctrine of the unity of opposites, for now we can say: 'the river: unchanging in its change, same and not the same', leaving it to the reader to evade or embrace the ostensible contradiction. And this interpretation shares the attractive features of its rival, since this combination of opposites in identity likewise exemplifies nature's paradoxically concealing itself.

On balance, I favour this alternative, since it not only ascribes a fruitful identity theory to Heraclitus, but also has the major advantage of implicating that theory in the *logos* of unified opposites.[21] So as with contradiction, here too we have a case study of intervening in the tradition in order to uncover an earlier stage, subsequently hidden by later versions of Heraclitus. I have illustrated some of the principles we invoke when reaching such judgements: which doctrine is more attractive and might contribute better to the global project of the thinker in question? If not consistent with all the evidence, does some of it speak in its favour? Can the recalcitrant or incompatible doxography be explained as creative exaggeration or misreading of the original theory, possibly premissed on writings which were even then incomplete (in the first instance by Heracliteans like Cratylus)? And again, we don't lose out, since we shall do philosophy with the Heraclitus of universal flux in the next chapter.

In conclusion we return to where we started: isn't Heraclitus a dreadful philosopher? When all is said on his behalf, even if we clear him of the Platonic and Aristotelian accusations concerning incoherent contradiction and so forth,[22] why did he expose himself to them – for surely his 'oracular' style is the root of the problem, laying him open to multiple misreadings? Why all those riddles, the paradoxes, all that ambiguity?

'The lord whose oracle is in Delphi neither speaks out nor conceals, but gives a sign' (KRS 244). To my mind, this is the most important and interesting single saying of Heraclitus to survive. What is he suggesting? Or rather, what sign is he giving us? First, apply the lessons you have learnt about opposites. You might have thought – too hastily – that speech and silence are mutually exclusive alternatives; and then have wondered how they might be unified. One who gives signs simultaneously manifests these opposites in the cryptic manner of oracular pronouncements, which are not explicit and unambiguous, in the way traffic signals are. Consider the traditional view of oracles, as documented in Herodotus. A king wonders whether it is safe to invade a neighbouring country, and consults the oracle. Answer: 'if you cross the river, a great kingdom will fall'. He does – and is vanquished, losing all.

Did the oracle lie? No: by invading his neighbour, the king did bring it about that a great kingdom fell – the oracle neither stated nor so much as implied which one. If the king wrongly inferred that it was his enemy's, that was his own fault. It is characteristic of oracular pronouncements on the traditional view that they contain, but also conceal, the truth. Sometimes, as in this example, that is because of referential indeterminacy; this indeterminacy is not the product of ambiguity, but it could be. Heraclitus is talking about himself (which characteristically does not preclude the comment's also being a religious pronouncement referring to the Delphic oracle, message within message). He seems not to tell the truth; that is because he doesn't tell it straight out. But he has carefully concealed the truth; it is there for discovery, if only we interpret his polysemic message correctly. 'God is war peace': if you infer that god is a contradiction, so much the worse for you; if you work out that the *logos* sustains a global pattern of interrelated oppositions, so much the better.

But wouldn't it have been even better to say so clearly, explicitly, unambiguously? To revert to a question left hanging: is it that Heraclitus' message has to be ambiguous, because it concerns something inherently unclear; or is it that ultimately a clear message will emerge, but it's good for us to have to work our way through to clarity? Answer: both at once, I think. The structure of the *logos* is manifold, dynamic, vast; the holistic perspective is god's eye view, and at least the overwhelming majority of people cannot get there by transcending their limited and parochial perspectives. They see nothing of what is before them; and in their wake – not that Heraclitus need have had any inkling of this – crazy fans of contradiction and universal flux and champions of relativism have sadly misinterpreted the *logos* by taking part of the message for the whole; only the select few read the oracles aright. And an explicit and unambiguous theory would be useless. 'Listening not to *me*, but to the *logos*,[23] it is wise to agree that all things are one.' Heraclitus knows he is an impressive figure (excessive self-deprecation is not one of his vices); he perceives the danger that you'll go about spouting his *dicta*, but won't have understood and internalised their import. Since his philosophy requires prolonged meditation on its difficult implications, deliberate and provocative obscurity is a help, not a hindrance. The appropriately paradoxical twist to his dialectic is that he gives what is worth having by withholding it.

A last word. As is customary, I have referred throughout to the 'fragments' of Heraclitus. In an obvious sense, what we have of him is indeed fragmentary: we don't know how to arrange what follows fragment 1, and some unknowable quantity of his book is missing. But in an appropriately hidden sense, what we have are *not* fragments. I mean this: where are the arguments? In a few instances Heraclitus does indicate what his argument is, by using Greek words which indicate that an inference is intended, and so forth. But much more of the time he expresses himself in gnomic aphorisms. By that I don't mean the triviality that, for example, 'the way up is the way down' is a pithy assertion. I don't know – no one knows – how much Heraclitus has disappeared, or in what order what we have was originally displayed. But I think I do know that there is no missing fragment in which he said: 'what do I mean by "the way up is the way down"? Well, let me clear that up for you . . . '. Heraclitus wants you to obey a hermeneutic injunction: construct the answer for yourself. The arguments have been left out on purpose. Each individual aphorism contains a concealed rationale; and they cumulatively amount to a great rational pattern, the *logos*; but all those arguments are for you to reproduce, in your own soul. Only then will you be able to say, with Heraclitus: 'I searched out myself' (KRS 246) – you will have reached the common truth by retreating from the common surface of things, executing a paradoxical and Heraclitean turn of thought. Anyway, that's how I read the signs.

Chapter 2

Refuting the irrefutable?

Before opening the *Theaetetus*, we should consider what doing philosophy with Plato is like. No one has had more philosophical progeny, major and minor: Aristotle – himself the master of legion Aristotelians – the Academic sceptics, the Stoics, Middle and Neo-Platonists, Schopenhauer (to name just one post-antique philosopher), all in their own very different ways are heirs to his legacy. And artists from Michelangelo to Shelley and Baron Corvo have drawn inspiration from his ideas. How can this be, when, for example, Aristotle in many writings takes Plato to task, or the sceptical Academy's methodology of commitment-free argument could hardly be more different from the baroque edifice of Neo-Platonic metaphysics? Sometimes, even when a later philosopher works for the wholesale rejection of a predecessor's (ostensible) conclusions, the questions which were raised remain in place, so that the predecessor's perceived agenda is carried forward. Thus Aristotle does much of his philosophy within a Platonic matrix. In the *Sophist*, there is an argument directed against 'Giants', who believe that nothing but bodies exist. The Stoics are extreme materialists, who contend that the soul and the virtues are bodies (in the *Sophist*, it was that very contention which served as a *reductio ad absurdum* of materialism), so how can they be located in the Platonic line of descent? The *Sophist* also formulates a criterion for saying that something exists, that it is such to act or be acted upon. Stoic causal theory argues that only bodies can enter causal relations;[1] thus they take advantage of one part of the dialogue to discard another. The possibility of following Plato into either scepticism or grand metaphysics arises not so much from which portion of a dialogue or dialogues one accepts to the exclusion of others, as from divergent global attitudes to what the dialogues are, and how they should be read.

What *are* Platonic dialogues? Some of them read just like the unadorned script of a play: named speakers exchange lines (there is no *dramatis personae* telling us something about the speakers or explicit stage directions, although the speeches invariably convey something of the setting and action). Others are much more elaborate; although they are still scripts, there is a narrator or set of narrators who recount a conversation which occurred in the past, sometimes the distant past; and this 'core' dialogue might be only partially or imperfectly 'reproduced' (the *Theaetetus* is an example of this format, although unlike, say, the *Symposium*, the narrator insists that his transcript is full and accurate). Plato himself is conspicuous by his absence (the only times he is so much as mentioned is when Socrates in the *Apology* includes him in the list of those willing to stand surety for the penalty imposed on him by the jury; and when a character in the *Phaedo* remarks that Plato could not be present at Socrates' death, as if to underline that the author *isn't* there in his writings, even on so poignant an occasion). And, taken together, the dialogues constitute a real corpus. By that I mean that they are bound together by connections ranging from plain cross-references to veiled allusions. That is a fact beyond dispute, and one which looms large in the history of writing: Plato and his contemporary and rival Isocrates, a rhetorical theorist, were the first Greek thinkers to compose such intellectual packages which convey meaning through the relations between their components.

As I said in the last chapter, some readers of Plato are convinced that the corpus encapsulates a set of complementary positive doctrines ('unitarians'); others claim to detect phases within Platonic philosophy, as one or another recommended method, type of argument or theory is replaced by another, occasionally incompatible, position ('developmentalists'). These conflicts cluster about the role of Socrates – does a 'Socratic' Socrates, viz a representation of the historical figure, give way before a 'Platonic' Socrates, viz a mouthpiece for a spectacular expansion of his interests? – and allegiance to the transcendental Forms. In such dialogues as the *Phaedo* and the *Republic* Socrates argues for and about these Forms. Above and beyond these equal sticks, there is Equality Itself: while this stick is equal to that one, but not another, Equality is absolutely and nothing but equal; while this person or theory is more beautiful than another, they are imperfectly so, in contrast to Beauty itself, which exemplifies (or perhaps somehow models without instantiating) perfect beauty. To know what f is, is to know the Form F; and since the Forms are eternal and incorporeal, understanding them demands liberating the soul, itself incorporeal and immortal, from the trammels of the body. But in the first part of the dialogue the *Parmenides*, Parmenides launches a sustained attack on the Theory of Forms, which Socrates cannot fend off. Unitarians believe that Parmenides' arguments are specious, and the point of the exercise is to clear up misunderstandings, so that the original theory emerges unscathed; some developmentalists feel that these arguments signal the need to modify the original theory in significant respects; yet others view the *Parmenides* as Plato's forthright abandonment of the theory. If the *Theaetetus* seeks to define knowledge, and knowledge comes from the Forms, why are they not mentioned? For some, Plato had not yet developed the theory; for others, he had already abandoned it; for others, the reader is intended to supply a missing Formal epistemology, realising that all the answers are to be found there; for others, the theory is simply irrelevant to the dialogue's questions, so nothing follows either way about its status. No one has won acceptance as having the better of the debate.

And no one is ever likely to, although of course fashions in Platonic scholarship, as in all else, change. What is responsible for this impasse? Simply that the dialogues are dialogues, with an absent author. All these readers, with the exception of the sceptics, are convinced that there is a substantive Platonic philosophy which the dialogues document: the fight is over what that philosophy is, and whether it evolves over time. Against this whole way of reading Plato there is another possibility: not sceptical as such, but 'open'. Why did Plato write dialogues? They are such supreme masterpieces that it is easy to overlook this question. But, before Plato, there were only philosophical poems and prose treatises; after Plato, although writers like the young Aristotle, Cicero, Berkeley and Hume emulated his practice with mixed success, the philosophical dialogue is a lonely exception to the expository rule of the argumentative treatise. We simply don't know where Plato found his antecedents, if any; many people have been tempted by the hypothesis that his model was Athenian tragedy and comedy[2] – after all, the dialogues are dramatic scripts – but no one has succeeded in demonstrating that they follow contemporary theatrical conventions, that the workings of the Athenian stage have analogues in Platonic writing.

It must have something to do with the historical Socrates, since we know that after his death Plato was not alone in composing Socratic *logoi*, dramatic representations of Socrates' words and deeds (this was a flourishing genre, but only the works of Plato himself and those of Xenophon, which give us a moralistic and intellectual but pedestrian Socrates, survive in more than fragments). But why Socrates should have stimulated this remarkable generic innovation is obscure – unless we rest content with the cliché that such was the force of his personality, etc., that his captivated disciples, Plato among them, were driven to construct Socratic memorials, especially because his reputation had been besmirched by the Athenian court's monstrous condemnation. But perhaps this can be made more than a cliché. In the Introduction, I described Greek philosophy as more than an 'academic' pursuit, as a way of life. We know that Socrates lived the philosophical life with a single-minded determination that to his detractors was unhealthily and destructively fanatical; maybe his adherents were so impressed by this pure devotion that they were galvanised into offering us 'living' versions of the philosopher *non pareil*, a sort of saint to emulate, as best we might. Why is Plato's absence mentioned in the *Phaedo*? A doctrinal answer: the dialogue argues that death is nothing more than the separation of immortal soul from mortal body, so that the real Socrates has not perished, and his follower Plato has not lost him (permanently). An 'open' answer: the dialogue's author keeps what is best in Socrates alive by giving us a paradigm of the philosophical life, and so need not bid him farewell.

If you believe in the doctrinal Plato, then you suppose the inspirational Socrates is his vehicle for conveying theses to which he is committed *in propria persona*. If you are not a Platonic devotee, you will deprecate this tactic; Socrates is a mere mouthpiece broadcasting the party line, as Plato devotes his literary genius to tarting up his favourite doctrines, using his rhetorical powers to endow them with the personal prestige of the seductive Socrates. If you are a fan of Plato, there is no (or little) overt or covert rhetorical manipulation: true, Socrates (and others) speak for the author, but they speak in arguments; and we are indeed meant to become doctrinal Platonists, but only because we have comprehended these authoritative arguments and appreciated their force (this is not unrelated to the explanation of Heraclitus' 'oracular' style). 'Open' reading is a radical alternative. Open readers take what they perceive to be the implications of the dialogue format, of the author's absence, with utmost seriousness. For them, there are no endorsed arguments, full stop: neither Socrates nor any other character is to be identified with Plato. If neither offshoots of the Athenian theatre nor meant to be acted out on stage, the dialogues are nevertheless to unfold within your mental theatre; and, since this is not *agitprop*, none of the contending voices is Plato's own, there is no ventriloquism. This approach does not entail that Plato is a cipher; we know what topics mesmerised him – they are the themes of the dialogues – what he considered promising (and distinctly unpromising) arguments about them – they are attacked and defended in the dialogues – and the importance he attached to their investigation, as witnessed by his heroic portrait of Socrates. What we do not and cannot know is what his own Platonism consisted in. This would be a retreat into an isolation far beyond the hiddenness of the Heraclitean *logos* – why this impenetrable self-concealment? Heraclitus' faith in his discovery of the truth never falters. Maybe Plato likewise fully trusted his convictions, but was even more sensitive than Heraclitus to the dangers of laziness and prostration before authority, to the extent that no authorial *imprimatur* is to be found, at any level. Or maybe he really was something of a sceptic before the letter: not persuaded that the truth cannot be ascertained, but unsure that he had hold of it.[3]

I am an 'open' reader of Plato. When you read Platonic dialogues, you must never forget that the only proper reaction to his dialectic is constantly to ask: 'where's the argument? Should the interlocutor have conceded that point to Socrates? There's a fallacy: perhaps so far from wishing to trick me, Plato's intention is that I see what's gone wrong, and begin to compose an alternative dialogue in my head. Or is it that Plato himself made a mistake?'. You cannot be supine; Plato incessantly demands an active and engaged reader. The dialogues function as dialectical templates. They are representations of people doing philosophy which get *you* to do philosophy; that, if you like, is how Plato pulls off the unparalleled trick of engaging you in philosophical conversation from beyond the grave – without uttering a word in his own voice.

In the sequel I shall try to give you a demonstration of active and 'open' reading (which you are not meant to take as authoritative!). Ideally, we would read through a dialogue in its entirety, since the individual episodes are always so combined that there is inevitably a considerable loss when one studies a selection; but that would be a book in itself. We shall restrict ourselves to the stretch of the *Theaetetus* which expounds and then demolishes the 'secret doctrine' of Heraclitus and Protagoras, since we thereby build on our work in the last chapter; and even within these limits our treatment will be highly selective. But you should learn what you can from the exercise, and then read all of the *Theaetetus* (and other dialogues).

A word of warning. For quite some time now there has been a widespread reaction against excessively 'analytical' interpretations of Plato, where what is deprecated is concentration on the reconstruction and dissection of argument to the exclusion of all else. There is much justice in the protest; an interpretation which rips an argument out of its dialectical context, making it completely anonymous, must be defective, since the thrust of the argument has everything to do with the further dialectical commitments of the interlocutor to whom it is attributed. But this fully justified demand for inclusive reading can spill over into a wrongheaded advocacy of 'literary' reading of Plato. No one in their right mind would deny that the Platonic dialogues are consummate literary artefacts – which is to say no more than that they are examples of extremely skilful writing. And it is perfectly true that, in addition to passages of dry, thorny dialectic, many (not all) dialogues also contain what are labelled as non-argumentative 'myths', abound in the most subtle characterisation and personal interaction, invest gesture, movement and other aspects of stage-setting with significance, incorporate vivid analogies and images, and are plausibly read as encrypting various messages by means of dazzling symbolic schemes.

To write all this off as mere window-dressing for the attractive display of argument is indeed a vulgar mistake. But to infer that the 'literary' material somehow works independently of the argument, that Plato is sometimes arguing, sometimes about some other business, is no less mistaken. A popular form of the 'literary' tendency is the supposition that the presentation and evaluation of character motivate Plato: he wrote dialogues because he wanted to show us how people's important convictions mould character and shape lives, and the best way to do that is to have his (semi-)fictional creations act out these beliefs. Again, there is a valuable intuition here, that Plato is wedded to the representation of doing philosophy as living an authentic life; one's philosophical commitments have ramifications which extend far beyond the confines of the study. Where the intuition sometimes goes wrong is in succumbing to the temptation to displace the argument from centre stage; all the 'literary' factors serve to sharpen our understanding of where the argument is going (and of where it has failed to reach). And since, on an 'open' reading, the process of argumentation is often as important as the conclusion of any given argument, creating full-blooded dialectical encounters also makes perfect sense. But for Plato, no less than for any other real philosopher, the argument itself is always the first and last thing.

Theaetetus: 'It seems to me that a man who knows something perceives what he knows, and the way it appears at present, at any rate, is that knowledge is simply perception' (*Theaetetus* 151E).[4] Why would Plato have Theaetetus say that? You might readily agree that the nature of knowledge is an obvious, and obviously important, issue for philosophers; but isn't this a glaringly misplaced stab at definition? For if I say 'I know that the square on the hypotenuse of a right-angled triangle equals the sum of the squares on the other two sides', or 'I know that Julius Caesar was murdered', or 'I know that raising interest rates will curb inflation', I am not claiming to perceive that these things are so: mathematical competence, retrospective historical knowledge and predictive economic expertise are not to be equated with perceptual experience. So isn't Plato setting up a straw man for Socrates to knock down? No. Don't I use a diagram to prove the Pythagorean theorem? I have never met Caesar, but could I know the circumstances of his death, in the absence of eyewitness testimony? What verifies my prediction, if not the subsequent evidence of our senses?

You might feel that these examples go to show that knowledge *involves* perception, but not that knowledge *is* nothing but perception. And you would be right: epistemology, the branch of philosophy which investigates knowledge and belief, explores mathematical reasoning, testimony and evidence. Empiricist epistemology contends that knowledge is grounded in perceptual experience. What is this 'grounding'? To ward off immediate counter-examples such as the ones I have supplied, sensible empiricists do not pretend that all knowing simply *is* seeing, etc.; instead they argue that all knowledge rests on a foundation of sense perception, and that foundation is very secure, perhaps incorrigible. Empiricists and their opponents argue over the nature and purported certainty of the perceptual foundation, and the possibility of building the rest of the edifice of knowledge upon it. This live debate is central to epistemology, and the *Theaetetus* is its richest and most influential founding text.

So Theaetetus' candidate definition is not silly and uninteresting, but it does cry out for expansion and analysis; and that is just what happens, for Socrates immediately replies that his suggestion is nothing other than Protagoras' Measure doctrine ('he said the very same thing, only he put it in rather a different way', 152A). The remainder of the first part of the dialogue is spent explaining how this is so, bringing in Heraclitus as well, and eventually testing the fully articulated defintion. The road taken is not to a mild version of empiricism; rather, it is argued that if knowledge is to be defined as perception, then perception must be Protagorean, and the world perceived must be Heraclitean. The interlocutors will agree that this radical definition fails miserably, falling to a *reductio ad absurdum*: Theaetetus' definition can only be sustained by incorporating a theory of perception and the world perceived which entails, amongst other unacceptable consequences, that language is impossible; since language is possible, the definition is a failure. They proceed to the consideration of other possibilities, none of which succeed either; we are left in *aporia*. But along the way we learn much about what knowledge could and cannot be; and the first part of the dialogue is superlative for its demonstration of dialectic at work.

Socrates continues with the example of the wind to which different people react differently, and infers that, on the Measure doctrine, the wind in itself is neither cold nor not cold, but is for individuals as it appears to them. He generalises this result: 'there is nothing which in itself is just one thing: nothing which you could rightly call anything or any kind of thing'; despite what we say, nothing 'is', but rather everything is in constant change (152D – E). By having Socrates call this a 'secret' doctrine, Plato is most likely signalling that while rooted in the original Measure, the theory as described diverges from or goes beyond Protagoras' own. How is this consistent with 'he said the very same thing'? Remember from the Introduction that even when we do philosophy with a living partner, it can happen that the implications of a position might be at least partially opaque to its author; thus the justification for going beyond an original formulation. And it might be that a modified thesis can be brought into conjunction with others so as to create a new, synthetic theory; thus the justification for divergence ('only he put it in rather a different way'). Socrates' version sticks to perception, for now (in addition to temperature, his examples are large and small, heavy and light); and the criterion of truth is emphatically said to be the individual, not a group of people.

What is especially noteworthy is his explicit identification of *appearance* with perception (152B – C). *Phantasia*, the Greek for 'appearance', is a noun corresponding to a verb used to express equivalents of the English 'it appears to me that . . . ', 'it seems to me that . . . '. In that case, isn't the identification illicit? For how can I move legitimately from 'it appears to me that you have discovered a new proof of Pythagoras' Theorem' or 'it seems to me that inflation is bound to increase' to 'I *perceive* that you have discovered a new proof of Pythagoras' Theorem' or 'I *see* that inflation is bound to increase', where 'perceive' and 'see' are used in the strict sense of the words? Wouldn't that be to beg the question in favour of radical empiricism? But Socrates is not made to beg any questions: 'the appearing of things, then, is the same as perception, *in the case of hot and things like that*' (152C, emphasis added). The candidate definition of knowledge is perception. One test that an adequate definition must meet has to do with its scope: does the purported definition of X apply to everything we think of as an X? It is not the case that we hold all the pre-theoretical examples of X fixed, so that a definition which fails to apply across the board is disqualified; it would be a useful result to discover that some of them are not really X (Fool's Gold isn't gold), and to be able to adjudicate on borderline cases (a foetus is [not] a human being). But a definition which rules out star cases is a failure: if *that* doesn't count as an X, what could? So what Socrates is doing is getting us to think about whether *all* appearance can be assimilated to sensory appearance – if we are properly alert readers. The corporate option for the Measure doctrine is ignored – for the time being – since it is the individual, not the group, who has sense organs (that every member of a college has eyes doesn't imply that the college itself does too). 'Perception, then, is always of what is, and unerring – as befits knowledge' (152C). Perception might seem a non-starter as a definition of knowledge; don't you all too often misperceive things, while knowledge gets them right? What the definition requires to stand a chance is relativism, so that your perceptions will be invariably true – for you. Thus Theaetetus requires (a version of) Protagoras.

Why the addition of Heraclitean flux? The text is not altogether explicit, but we can reason out why this version of Protagoras requires a version of Heraclitus. The theory does not deny that there is an external world, i.e. say that there is nothing but subjective experience; rather, things interact with perceivers to generate their incorrigible experiences. Were the wind of an intrinsic and stable temperature, then how it *feels* to you might not be how it *is*. To eliminate this threat, the wind must always be just as it appears. But appearances – we think – conflict, not only in how they seem to different observers at the same time, but also to the same observer at different times. Therefore the only way to make all perceptions come out true, and so count at least as potential instances of knowledge, is to assume that what they are perceptions *of* obligingly become what they are perceived to be, in a perfect match; and, given the transience of perception, the corresponding flux will have to be total, to insulate each of the (not really) 'conflicting' appearances from error (this is fully worked out in 153E – 154B: the second and third parts of the dialogue discuss epistemological issues left unbroached in the first part). This delivers the final conjunction of the three theses, knowledge as perception needing relativism, which in turn needs flux.

As with relativism, so flux too might make you squeamish. On the objective side, if the wind isn't intrinsically cold, etc., is it anything at all? It certainly can't be anything perceptible; and if knowledge is perception, that would seem to entail that either the remaining nature of the wind is unknowable, or that it is a something close to nothing, the blank causal postulate factored in as what lies 'behind' our experiences. Neither option is at all palatable. On the subjective side, a thing 'doesn't always appear the same even to yourself because you never remain the same as yourself' (154A): if *you* are nothing above and beyond the subject of occurrent sense impressions, changing as and when they so frequently do, don't you dissolve into innumerable, evanescent successors? And it is not simply that 'the verb "to be" must be totally abolished': 'such words as "something", "of something", or "mine", "this" or "that", or any other name that makes things stand still' (157B) are improper, since, it is assumed, their use implies that there are stable objects to which they refer. But, you might well wonder, what linguistic resources remain once the offending terms are abolished; how can we establish reference to what exists only more or less instantaneously? Plato intends you to be very quizzical, although the ultimate refutation of the definition will not focus directly on quite these implications for ontology and personal identity. Platonic dialogues abound with unusual and outrageous arguments; it is very far from the case that Socrates condemns *outré* ideas as such. What flies in the face of common sense might be what we *should* believe – if it survives dialectical assay. So this amazing explanation of how things appear will have its chance in the dialectical arena. The phenomenon of conflicting appearances has constantly exercised philosophers (you should be able to see that Protagoras' wind is a cousin of Heraclitus' seawater; and the Sceptics skilfully appealed to these appearances for their own ends, as we shall see in the next chapter). The dialectic of the *Theaetetus* supplies our best example of a relativistic reaction to these ostensible conflicts.

The critical examination begins with a scornful question: why not '"pig is the measure of all things" or "baboon" or some yet more out-of-the-way creature with the power of perception'? Such substitutions – and add Heraclitean fish – would have made it uncomfortably obvious that 'wise' Protagoras is 'in reality no better authority than a tadpole – let alone any other man' (161C – D). (These remarks are addressed not to Theaetetus, but to Theodorus, Theaetetus' expert teacher in mathematics and said by Socrates to be Protagoras' friend: why bother seeking such tuition, if all appearances are true? How can Protagoras have any 'friends', if interpersonal communication can be no more than momentary encounters between fugitive selves? This is typical of Plato: collaborating with the overt challenge to a relativist's claiming authority are 'literary' features of the characterisation designed to get you deeper into the dialectic.) You might wonder whether the question is fair: mightn't Protagoras suggest that each species perceives in its own way, and then argue either that human senses are superior, or that 'man is the measure (for men)', 'pig is the measure (for pigs)', etc. (later even sensitive plants are measures for themselves [167B])? Of course, none of that would show that *Protagoras* is a privileged knower, and Socrates warns that relativism imperils philosophy itself, the search for knowledge: 'to examine and try to refute each other's appearances and judgements, when each person's are correct – this is surely an extremely tiresome piece of nonsense, if the *Truth* of Protagoras is true' (161E).[5] This is an accusation pregnant with significance. First, we wrongheadedly attempt to engage in philosophical dialectic: if 'each person's appearances and judgements are correct', what about our conviction that this argument is invalid, that one sound? If that conviction is mistaken, so much for the thesis that man is the measure. But if that conviction is true – for us – then it cannot be that a solitary individual is always the criterion, since dialectic demands the logical *agreement* of the interlocutors; so if it seems to us that we are doing philosophy, we philosophers working together are the criterion (never mind that in 'I see a fallacy lurking' I'm not using my eyes). Second, what is the meaning of 'true' in 'the *Truth* of Protagoras is true'? 'True for . . . ' whom? The urgency of these questions will be driven home in the following assault on relativism.

You needn't wonder on your own what Protagoras might have had to say in his defence; for Socrates offers to impersonate the relativist. 'Protagoras' insists: 'when you are examining any doctrine of mine by the method of question and answer, if the person being questioned answers as I myself would answer, and gets caught, then it is I who am refuted; but if his answers are other than I should give, then it is he who is put in the wrong' (166A). 'Gets caught', 'am refuted', 'put in the wrong': this indignant and voluble Protagoras has no qualms about acknowledging the possibility of dialectical examination, and takes it for granted that such a procedure – if conducted fairly – reveals winners and losers. Since neither the real Protagoras nor the Protagoras of the *Theaetetus* is a fool – assuming anyone could be foolish or wise, by his lights – Plato's Protagoras, it must be assumed, has some way of trying to reconcile 'all appearances are true' with dialectical self-defence. Will the attempted reconciliation prove well-founded or spurious?

The riposte is spirited and detailed, spelling out whatever implications of the position had remained implicit (e.g. there are 'an infinite number of men coming to be in succession, assuming this process of becoming unlike', 166B; 'each man's perceptions are . . . his own private events', 166C). However: 'the man whom I call wise is the man who can change the appearances – the man who in any case where bad things both appear and are for one of us, works a change and makes good things appear and be for him' (166D); and 'for each person and each city, things are what they seem to them to be' (168B) – corporate measures are admitted, and the appearances include social judgements, not only immediate sense experience. This should remind you of one of the possibilities I floated for the historical Protagoras in the last chapter (not a coincidence, since I was tapping into the *Theaetetus*). If we are all knowers, there are nevertheless privileged experts, whose expertise resides in their ability to ameliorate unfortunate appearances. 'It seems to me that I'm badly off.' 'No, listen: true, you haven't much money, but . . . ' And the depression lifts. What is the relativistic analysis of the result of this change? Is it: (i) it is good for you not to think that you are badly off; or (ii) it seems to you that you are not badly off, and that feels good? On (ii), that things *are* good or bad falls within the scope of the Measure doctrine, but not on (i). Both analyses have their pluses and minuses. (i) would of course oblige Protagoras to retreat from unrestricted relativism, since a range of objective value judgements would be immune from relativisation; but they would supply a supporting framework within which we might adjust our true appearances. (ii) preserves the undiluted Measure doctrine, but leaves mysterious how one might become and remain an authority: is it just a brute, contingent fact that, for example, most of us regard pain as a bad thing, and praise the doctor who can relieve it? Why are the words Plato puts into Protagoras' mouth indeterminate on this important score? Two compatible possibilities. First, he is not setting up a straw man, sophistically hoping that you will overlook the difference between (i) and (ii); the choice between them arises in the tacit dialectic between the dialogue's author and its intelligent readers. Second, as I suggested, perhaps the historical Protagoras expressed himself indeterminately, and Plato is advancing the tradition by indicating where choices must be made. Of course, there is always the third (highly unlikely) possibility that Plato was innocently insensitive to whether 'good' and 'bad' fall within the scope of the Measure doctrine. But even then, an acute reader of the dialogue can grasp what its author overlooked; if Plato saw some of what Protagoras missed, maybe you can do the same for Plato, adding to his 'footnotes'. That is how philosophy is done.

Socrates comes back to finish Protagoras off. Protagoras had berated him for indulging in disgraceful logic-chopping and other cheap tricks, and he cautions Theodorus: 'now there is one kind of mistake I want you to be specially on your guard against, namely, that we do not unconsciously slip into some childish form of argument. We don't want to get into disgrace for this again' (169C). This is a good example of the complex dialogues which go on between the characters and between Plato and you. The real Protagoras cannot be there.[6] On one level, the character Socrates is saying to his interlocutors: 'some of what precedes misses the target; what follows is meant to be decisive' (whether his concession to Protagoras is serious or ironic is not at all obvious). On another level, the author Plato is saying to you the reader: 'there is my character Socrates' assessment of the dialectical situation – see if you accept it'.

Pace Protagoras, '*all* men' (170A) believe that wisdom and ignorance exist, and that the difference between these cognitive states arises from whether they involve true or false judgement. Hence an exquisite dilemma. The first horn. Assume that all judgement is true (the relativist claim). Then, since there are plenty of people who sincerely believe that many opinions are false, and that belief, on relativism, must be true, it is true that some appearances are false. The second horn. Simply assume that not all judgement is true: relativism is immediately refuted. Since, necessarily, either all judgement is true or not all judgement is true, relativism is untenable. You might say to yourself: 'I have just been braced up to be a rigorous and honest dialectician. Is this dilemma a dilemma *for Protagoras*? In the last chapter, I read that, on a relativistic theory, the truth predicate comes with hyphens, it is itself relativised. We have been attentive to the meaning of "true" so far, and must continue to be so. There are two choices. If "true" as it occurs in the dilemma is absolute, then this is flagrant question-begging. But if "true" is relativistic – as it should be, in fairness to Protagoras – the dilemma's conclusion yields, at best: "it is true-for-Protagoras that it is true-for-me that truth is absolute" – and why should that bother him? He has the opportunity to make me change my mind; not to replace a false belief with a true one, but rather to change inferior appearances for better ones, since it seems to him that adherence to relativism is a good thing. And that seems consistent to me'.

The *Theaetetus* addresses this nagging worry, although just how the dialectic operates, and whether it avoids the charge of question-begging, is one of the most difficult and interesting issues in Platonic interpretation.[7] The exchange must be quoted in full:

Socrates: And what of Protagoras himself? Must he not say this, that supposing he himself did not believe that man is the measure, any more than the majority of people (who indeed do not believe it), then this *Truth* which he wrote is true for no one? On the other hand, suppose he believed it himself, but the majority of men do not agree with him; then you see – to begin with – the more those to whom it does not seem to be the truth outnumber those to whom it does, so much the more it isn't than it is?

Theodorus: That must be so, if it is going to be or not be according to the individual judgement.

Socrates: Secondly, it has this most exquisite feature: Protagoras admits, I presume, that the contrary opinion about his own opinion (namely, that it is false) must be true, seeing he agrees that all men judge what is.

Theodorus: Undoubtedly.

Socrates: And in conceding the truth of the opinion of those who think him wrong, he is really admitting the falsity of his own opinion?

Theodorus: Yes, inevitably.

Socrates: But for their part the others do not admit that they are wrong?

Theodorus: No.

97

Socrates:	But Protagoras again admits *this* judgement to be true, according to his written doctrine?
Theodorus:	So it appears.
Socrates:	It will be disputed, then, by everyone, beginning with Protagoras – or rather, it will be admitted by him, when he grants to the person who contradicts him that he judges truly – when he does that, even Protagoras himself will be granting that neither a dog nor the 'man in the street' is the measure of anything at all which he has not learnt. Isn't that so?
Theodorus:	It is so.
Socrates:	Then since it is disputed by everyone, the *Truth* of Protagoras is not true for anyone at all, not even for himself?
Theodorus:	Socrates, we are running my friend too hard.
Socrates:	But it is not at all clear, my dear Theodorus, that we are running off the right track.

(170E – 171C)

The passage begins with Socrates' frank admission that, to bite as deeply as possible, the refutation must wring the concession that relativism is false from Protagoras *himself* ('supposing he himself did not believe that man is the measure'). The alternative, that if he sticks to his guns the Measure doctrine will be (much more) false than true, is not powerful, since a 'wise' Protagorean expert chuffs himself on the rarity of his wisdom. The 'exquisite feature' is the claim that the following argument is a self-refutation. Why? Measure is a doctrine about beliefs. The argument turns on an application of Measure to special beliefs – beliefs about Measure – to infer that Measure is false for everybody. The logic of self-refutation fascinates philosophers, both because it is so unusual, and since to convict an opponent of it is the ultimate knock-down refutation: what could be easier and more gratifying than to deal with people who blow themselves out of the water?[8] But why must Protagoras admit that 'the contrary opinion about his own opinion . . . must be true'? What has happened to the qualifiers? He must admit that the contrary opinion must be *true-for-Socrates*, etc., and where's the harm in that? Or in conceding not 'the falsity of his own opinion', but rather that his opinion is false-for-others? And so on throughout. The qualifiers have vanished; but isn't their disappearance a cheat, so that Protagoras remains immune to refutation? We should avoid the conclusion that Plato has simply been negligent, since he is hardly unaware of the dialectical obligation to relativise the truth predicate;[9] evidently he believes that something licenses the switch to absolute truth, but has concealed the justification. Are we 'running Protagoras too hard'? Why should we accept Socrates' reassurance that the question has not been begged?

That is for you to decide, by doing more Greek philosophy in Plato's company. This chapter's title is a question because it does not tell you whether positions such as Protagorean relativism are really accessible to refutation;[10] but here is a thought to be getting on with, for you to build on. Socrates claims to have done his best to speak for Protagoras, letting him (sort of) into the conversation despite the danger that relativism about truth might pose to the very activity of dialectic. Let us scrutinise that danger more closely. A cagy Protagoras will always be saying things like 'yes, it is true-for-me that it-is-true-for-you that . . . but . . . '. Is that to be *saying* anything at all? If we believe that to assert proposition *P* is to commit oneself to its unrelativised truth, why should *we* concede that a consistent assertion of relativism is even possible, let alone true-for . . . ? Were such a reaction reasonable, then relativism, so far from being irrefutable, would be resoundingly refuted, because incoherent (which is not to say that it has 'the exquisite feature' as such). Or perhaps we should retreat somewhat: it's not that relativists cannot so much as speak amongst themselves – we remain agnostic on that question – but we deny them access to our dialectic, since its underpinning in absolute assertion excludes them from taking part in our discourse.[11] Were that the case, relativism would prove to be irrefutable without begging the question – but should we lose any sleep over that?

You might have thought that with the disposal of Protagoras (remember that the difficulties for relativism we canvassed were not confined to the possibility of self-refutation; and we are skipping over much else, such as how a Protagorean might account for future-directed true appearances), Theaetetus' definition would be immediately consigned to the rubbish, since it depends on relativism; if relativism is not viable, neither is the definition of knowledge as perception.[12] But remember the full structure: relativism in its turn depends on Heraclitean flux, and we shall complete our investigation of the *Theaetetus* by inspecting Socrates' refutation of that thesis, since it is one of our running themes. Socrates begins by reminding us that the theory postulates *total* flux; therefore everything must change *constantly* in *every* respect (181E: e.g. things are not only always moving about through space, but also changing colour, temperature, etc.). 'We were most anxious to prove that all things are in change, in order to make that answer [viz knowledge is perception] come out correct; but what has really emerged is that, if all things are in change, every answer, on whatever subject, is equally correct, both "it is thus" and "it is not thus" – or if you like "becomes", as we don't want to use any expressions which will bring our friends to a stand-still' (183A). That is bad enough, since 'thus-and-not-thus' is contradictory; and, as we have seen, contradictions are ineffable and incredible. But there is worse to come: ' . . . except that I said "thus" and "not thus". One must not use even the word "thus"; for this "thus" would no longer be in change; nor yet "not thus" for here again there is no change. The exponents of this theory need to establish some other language . . . ' (183A – B). How could they manage that? There could be no language without reference; but totally pervasive flux does away with anything which persists even fleetingly to which one might refer; so, even were the Heraclitean theory true, it would be inexpressible and unbelievable. This is a very neat counterpoint to the Protagoras who is either incoherent or to be ignored as *hors de combat*; beside him we set, and set aside, the Heraclitus who must remain silent, on pain of refuting his own doctrine by giving it (static) expression.

We now leave Plato, whose dialogues are prolific with drama-tised dialectic, for the austere experience of reading Aristotle. But if it's all footnotes to Plato, Aristotle is *the* philosopher's philosopher; taken together, his thoughts are the most imposing and profound philosophical system ever created. Unlike Plato, Aristotle is directly committed to his arguments and theories; but is it right to say that they add up to a grand system? Although there is no Aristotelian analogue to the Socratic Question, here we encounter something like the developmentalist/unitarian debate. For the Aristotelian corpus consists of so-called 'esoteric' treatises, that is, lecture notes and other work not prepared for publication ('publication' in the ancient world was a matter of copying manuscripts for circulation). If not for external con-sumption, we cannot expect them to be reader-friendly: they need not have the (relative) lucidity of documents intended for others, since Aristotle himself could make do with a compressed, opaque and possibly lacunose record for his own private under-standing; arguments might be provisional; an *aporia* might be less than serious, or its solution only *pro tem*. Furthermore, dif-ferent bits of the corpus seem to be saying different things – on some readings, incompatible things (for example, the ontology of the *Categories* and the central books of the *Metaphysics*). Aristotelian developmentalists believe that his philosophy evolved, from an immature 'Platonic' period to a maturity itself containing distinct phases, and that it perhaps never achieved finality. Aristotelian unitarians argue for reconciling works which, if not always saying the same thing, express complemen-tary doctrines.[13] All Aristotelians were unitarians until the nine-teenth century; from antiquity through the Middle Ages until that break, it was taken entirely for granted that this philosophy was a comprehensive system. But even a developmentalist who denies this has to concede that, if not a system, Aristotelian phil-osophy is *systematic*; it all hangs together to an impressive, indeed unique, degree. This creates an embarrassment for the new reader: where to begin? For example, the *Poetics*' importance in the history of literary criticism is second to none; it is a short (actually incomplete) treatise, so why not start there – surely Aristotle's aesthetic theory must be relatively free-standing? If you try that, you will find that one of its criteria for literary excellence is organic unity; to understand that, you must turn to Aristotle's *Physics* and biological works; to understand them, you must make sense of his doctrines of causation and explanation and of hylomorphism, the theory of form and matter; to do that, you must penetrate the *Metaphysics* – where hylomorphism receives various expositions, obscure in themselves and in their relations to one another . . . In sum, the Aristotelian corpus is a remarkable intellectual object, whose topology makes altogether unanticipated connections.

That notwithstanding, we shall plunge into *Metaphysics Gamma*, in which Aristotle subjects our cast of Presocratics and Sophists to his own style of dialectical examination. 'Metaphysics' originally and literally meant nothing more than 'after the *Physics*', which is where the editors who compiled the Aristotelian corpus placed these books. That they should be read after the works which precede them in the corpus as we have it is open to serious question; but that they belong together is not (although their interrelations are in some cases very problematic). The editorial decision was sound because in the *Metaphysics* Aristotle is engaged in what he calls 'first philosophy'. First philosophy is first because it studies the principles presupposed by secondary disciplines, philosophical, mathematical and scientific: what is being? Are some beings primary? On what principles and with what techniques must we investigate the world, in the light of our ontological findings? How is it possible to validate basic principles, if there is nothing more fundamental to which one might appeal? As with Plato, our Aristotelian exercise will be limited, restricted to his dialectical defence of the principle of contradiction against the now usual suspects; but again you should be able to move forth from *Metaphysics Gamma* into the further reaches of that amazing philosophical topology.

'It falls to the philosopher, i.e. the student of what is characteristic of all substance, also to investigate the principles of trains of reasoning' (1005b8).[14] Aristotle's ontology is pluralistic, viz he accepts that, for example, you, your skin colour, the species human being, the heavenly bodies, mathematical lines and numbers . . . all exist; and he also recognises the intellectual credentials of special disciplines devoted to their study, e.g. biology, astronomy, geometry, arithmetic, optics . . . These special disciplines are distinct because they apply proprietary modes of study to that part of being which falls within their competence. A mathematician when doing arithmetic manipulates numbers in accordance with arithmetical rules to discover proofs in accordance with the standards of mathematical practice, and these proofs are knowledge. But mathematicians in their role of mathematicians do not ask: what *is* a number? They take the existence of even and odd numbers for granted. They do indeed distinguish between good and bad proofs but do not ask: what makes proof possible? These are the tasks of the philosopher; the Aristotelian studies how the types of being are related, and what accordingly might justify the techniques of the specialist disciplines. (E.g. for Aristotle, while numbers exist, they do not do so independently of the substances which they characterise. Here is one book, there are three birds . . . The mathematician abstracts these quantitative predicates for study, although the numbers are not to be found on their own.) So it is not that the mathematicians and the others do not gain knowledge; but it is the philosopher alone who can fully see what they are doing. At a sufficient level of generality, it becomes apparent that there are certain rational principles ('the things which in mathematics are termed axioms', 1005a20) which 'hold good of every thing-that-is and not of a certain genus, separate and distinct from the others' (1005a22 – 3); only the philosopher will isolate and apprehend them in their full generality, in search of the most secure instruments of thought.

Aristotle claims that a single principle is the firmest of all: 'for the same thing to hold good and not to hold good simultaneously of the same thing and in the same respect is impossible (given any further specifications which might be added against the dialectical difficulties)' (1005b19 – 22).[15] Why should it be accorded that status? 'For it is impossible for anyone to believe that the same thing is and is not, as some consider Heraclitus said – for it is not necessary that the things one says one should also believe. But if it is not possible for contraries to hold good of the same thing simultaneously . . . and the opinion contrary to an opinion is that of the contradictory, then obviously it is impossible for the same person to believe simultaneously that the same thing is and is not; for anyone who made that error would be holding contrary opinions simultaneously' (1005b23 – 32). Note Aristotle's caution about the 'contradictory' Heraclitus. Why should such a belief be not odd or risible or lamentable – not simply erroneous – but *impossible*? The argument is that not all speech is the expression of belief. 'That is a charming outfit' – a social lie, since I really believe that you look a fright. But I could, of course, entertain that belief (you do). 'Star orange crazy to': no belief there, true or false, since a jumble of words says nothing. A minimal proposition must predicate some attribute of a subject, or deny that the subject possesses the predicate: 'X is . . . ', 'X is not . . . '. Of course we can conjoin beliefs: 'that is a charming outfit, and I bet it will not fall out of fashion'. So why not: 'that is a charming outfit, and it is not a charming outfit'? We do change our minds. Today I happily believe that my jacket is a beauty; after your withering remarks, I sadly conclude that its colours are garish. But I do not hold these contrary beliefs simultaneously; and the idea is that I could not do so. Why? There's a fool born every minute ('I'm sure to win the lottery', 'L. Ron Hubbard and his followers inhabit an astral plane' . . .): why shouldn't I suppose that contradictions cannot obtain, but allow that those who believe and utter them take the cake for stupidity?

Think of language as a game, in which the basic move is the utterance of a minimal assertion. I say, 'that is a charming outfit' – I have moved one of the game's counters forward. I say, 'that is not a charming outfit' – I pull it back. To say both at once would be to shift the counter forward and back simultaneously – have you ever seen anyone perform such a trick? The argument is that the linguistic analogue is equally impossible. To say P and compatible Q is to say two things; to pronounce P and not P is to say nothing at all. I can say the words, but I have told you nothing, since the conjuncts cancel each other out; I can try to think the thought, but one of the would-be beliefs erases the other: the combination is literally unthinkable. You might object: 'true, I don't catch people spouting "X is p and X is not p" as such; but I do think that they nevertheless entertain contradictory beliefs, albeit without asserting them as baldly as that. For example, someone might believe that John is honest; and, seeing the fellow over there pinch a wallet, sincerely utter "look at that thief!". Unbeknownst to the speaker, John is the pickpocket. But she hasn't relinquished her belief in John's virtue; so she simultaneously believes of John that he is honest and not honest. Again, people are inclined to deceive themselves, when the truth would be too hard to bear. I know a woman whose husband is dying of cancer, but is, as the saying goes, "in denial". Some days she speaks cheerfully of the vacation they'll take together in Australia next year, once he's recovered; on others, she discusses funeral arrangements. And sometimes she even passes from the one attitude to the other in mid-sentence. It seems to me that she simultaneously believes "he will die" and "he will not die"'.

Do these examples show that Aristotle is wrong? No, although their explanation is a philosophical challenge. In the first case, the speaker is ignorant of the fact that John and the thief are one and the same; granted, from the third-person perspective she is committed to contradictory propositions, but she is not so placed as to derive the contradiction for herself, and believe it (working out how the propositions remain isolated, despite their common reference to John, is far from easy). The second case is considerably more difficult. Does the poor wife really deceive herself and confront the harsh truth simultaneously? One can change one's mind very quickly: when she switches in mid-sentence, might it not be that she has shifted from the dream she stores in one part of her mind to the reality which threatens it, kept safely away in another mental compartment? Philosophers are not at all sure how self-deception and other kinds of irrationality are best analysed: what psychological mechanisms might effect transitions from one set of beliefs to another, incompatible one? But what is clear is that those plagued by such forms of irrationality 'don't add up', viz are in a mental state we cannot make ready sense of, precisely because our reason, if working properly, rejects contradiction, as Aristotle insists.

We right-thinking, rational people know that contradiction is beyond the pale; does that mean that we have seen the Heracliteans off, ruled them out of court – refuted them? Now we come to what is most interesting in Aristotle's view of the dialectical situation, what it permits, and does not. 'We have just *accepted* that it is impossible to be and not to be simultaneously, and we have *shown* by means of this that it is the firmest of all principles' (1006a3 – 5, emphasis added). On the basis of that acceptance and demonstration, can we not go on to refute the Heracliteans? 'Some, owing to lack of training, actually ask that it be demonstrated: for it is lack of training not to recognise of which things demonstration ought to be sought, and of which not' (1006a5 – 8), and nothing is less in need of demonstration than the principle of contradiction. Why should we agree? Let us distinguish between our considering whether or not to adopt a principle, and our attempting to impose it on those who either ignore or deny it. In the first case, if the principle is genuinely in question, we must hold it in abeyance while inspecting its validity; otherwise we are already committed to it, and the test is a sham. But if 'X is p and X is not p' is unthinkable, how could we put the principle on ice for the duration of the test? Any thinking, to be coherent, would have to steer clear of contradiction, and so would be assuming what was supposed to be established. Likewise in the second case, if a fair refutation must not assume the falsity of what is to be refuted from the outset, how can we *refute* the Heraclitean? For if our argument against him is to make sense, let alone be valid, it must obey the principle – it would seem we have begged the question. Any *reductio ad absurdum* argument works by deriving a contradiction, and demanding that the opponent abandon the premiss(es) which permit its derivation: how could this work against someone who believes – or, at any rate, seems to say – that contradiction is *not* absurd?

Disappointingly, although I have assembled this answer from the materials Aristotle provided, initially he takes a different tack: 'for in general it is impossible that there should be demonstration of everything, since it would go on to infinity so that not even so would it be demonstration' (1006a8 – 9). This is true, but irrelevant. ' – Why did you buy that jacket? – To look good. – Why do you want to look good? – What an odd question: to attract people. – Why do you want to attract people? – Go away.' In ordinary life we often demand that people justify themselves, or try to justify ourselves by supplying reasons for our beliefs and actions. And we take it for granted that a proffered explanation might itself cry out for further justification in its turn. But we become intolerant when our inquisitor refuses to leave off (in the above dialogue, the respondent is impatiently assuming that the propriety of the desire to attract others is self-evident – rightly or wrongly). But suppose we had all the time and patience in the world: need the provision of reason after reason ever come to an end? This is now a philosophical question. In the *Posterior Analytics*, where Aristotle for the first time in history develops a formal theory of demonstration, he argues that proof must ultimately reside upon indemonstrable starting-points. Otherwise one of two possibilities would have to obtain. Either, as here in *Metaphysics Gamma*, the chain of demonstration would be unending; but justification cannot be infinitely open-ended (compare a chandelier 'suspended' from a chain which does not end in a fixed bolt). Or the chain might be not infinite, but circular: we use *A* to prove *B*, *B* to prove *C*, *C* to prove *D* . . . , and eventually circle back to prove *A*. But if *A* requires some of its successors to be known by way of proof, it cannot licitly be used to prove them without begging the question. Since this exhausts the alternatives, indemonstrables must be accepted (you might wonder why then we should have any faith in them, or confidence in the proofs built on their foundations; Aristotle and others have offered answers, none of which are obviously satisfactory). But this isn't what we want to hear about the principle of contradiction; even if 'it is impossible that there should be demonstration of everything', why shouldn't the principle figure as the conclusion of a *finite* demonstration? The answer is that the principle would be presupposed by *any* proof, so that infinity is a red herring.

This turn down a blind alley – not at all a rare experience in reading Aristotle – was not unrewarding; but next he guides us firmly down the highway: 'but even this can be demonstrated to be impossible, in the manner of a refutation, if only the disputant says something. If he says nothing, it is ridiculous to look for a statement in response to one who has a statement of nothing, in so far as he has not; such a person, in so far as he is such, is similar to a vegetable' (1006a11 – 15). Shades of Protagoras the plant? What is 'saying nothing'? Remaining mute, or coming out with gibberish? Either way, there is nothing to refute. 'I mean something different from demonstrating, because in demonstrating one might be thought to beg the original [question], but if someone else is cause of such a thing it must be refutation and not demonstration. In response to every case of that kind the original [step] is not to ask him to state something either to be or not to be (for that might well be believed to beg what was originally at issue), but at least to signify something both to himself and to someone else; for that is necessary if he is to say anything. For if he does not, there would be no statement for such a person, either in response to himself or to anyone else. But if he does offer this, there will be demonstration, for there will already be something definite' (1006a15 – 25).[16] The dialectical game mirrors the linguistic game. Let the Heraclitean make the opening move. Let him move a counter, either asserting a proposition or denying one; then there will be 'something definite', 'definite' in that a given attribute is either predicated or denied of some given subject.[17] Then we are off and away, since these propositions exclude their contradictories. What if that is denied? Then this player has disqualified himself, by attempting impossible moves; if nothing definite is said by him, nothing need be said by us in refutation, since he has stopped playing.

This is to imagine a wayward dialectician at least some of whose statements are meaningful: what if he is hardcore? ' . . . He says nothing. For he says neither that it is so-and-so nor that it is not so-and-so, but that it is both so-and-so and is not so-and-so; and again he also *denies* both these, saying that it is nei-ther so-and-so nor not so-and-so. For if he did not, something would already be definite' (1008a31 – 4). If it doesn't sound like outright nonsense, that is only because we pay heed first to 'it is so-and-so', then to 'it is not so-and-so'; we are under no obliga-tion to take in and refute both at once, because then 'there is nothing definite'. If not refuted, that is not because we have failed to disprove what could be attacked. Some positions are irrefutable because demonstrably proven true; others are (cur-rently) unrefuted because we aren't smart enough; others are 'irrefutable' in scare-quotes because they are, as it were, below rather than above rational assault, not even a coherent target.

It is likely that reading through these selections from *Metaphysics Gamma* has not felt like reading the *Theaetetus*: Aristotle speaks for himself (often with a controlling arm about our shoulders, when he uses 'we'); and argument, objection and qualification are presented as a definitive argumentative sequence for our endorsement,[18] not as a dialectical matrix for the production of our own arguments as we negotiate with the dialogue. But you should also be able to detect the affinities between Plato and Aristotle. Both are exercised by intertwined issues to do with contradiction and the limits of meaningful communication; both flag up the need for dialectical propriety in the assessment of extreme doctrines, as Socrates does his best for Protagoras, and Aristotle warns us off question-begging. Reading them together will help you to appreciate that the Greek philosophical tradition derives much of its power and attraction from incorporating geniuses of different bent who nevertheless have dialectic in common, and make that tradition by arguing with and about one another. Now let us see how Aristotle applies his theoretical findings to the history of philosophy.

On Protagoras: 'if everything that is thought or imagined is true, it is necessary that everything should be simultaneously true and false; for many people have mutually contrary beliefs, and regard those whose opinions are not the same as their own as in error, so that it is necessary that the same thing should both be and not be. And if the latter, it is necessary that what is thought to be should all be true; for those who are in error and those who have the truth hold mutually opposite opinions, and so, if that is the state of things-that-are, all will have the truth' (1009a7 – 15). Your first reaction might be one of disappointment: how can this be an adequate diagnosis, when solipsistic relativism ducks contradiction altogether? But we should ask whether Aristotle is discussing the historical Protagoras, or the Protagoras of the *Theaetetus*. If the latter construct, then since the Measure doctrine entails flux, and flux does away with thought and communication, 'nothing definite has been said'. If the former, then this Protagoras should concede that 'many people have mutually contrary beliefs'; then, if the preceding discussion of the dialectical possibilities holds water, Aristotle has the right to invoke his analysis; were a solipsistic retreat beaten, he could ignore such a 'vegetable'.

On the Heracliteans: 'again, observing that all nature is in change, and that no truth is had about that which is in [process of] alteration, it was not possible to have the truth at least concerning that which is in [process of] every style and manner of alteration. This belief blossomed into the most extreme of all the opinions we have mentioned, that of those who proclaimed themselves Heracliteans; such as Cratylus, who in the end considered that he ought to say nothing, and merely moved his finger' (1010a7 – 13). Aristotle has two replies. First, he denies that a thing in change is (altogether) not what it is ceasing to be; second, he accuses the Heracliteans of wrongly generalising from what (they think) is the case 'in a minority even of perceptible things' (1010a26 – 7). Again one might feel restive with this diagnosis. Aristotle points out that since qualitative and quantitative change are distinct, that something is changing in the one respect doesn't mean that it is also changing in the other. But didn't the *Theaetetus* say in so many words that *everything* is changing in *every* way? And doesn't Aristotle recognise as much ('that which is in [process of] every style and manner of alteration'), and then blithely beg the question against the flux theorists in the next breath?

What sort of philosophical history is Aristotle doing here? On the one hand, the surrounding context suggests that he is consulting his *Theaetetus* (there is also discussion of conflicting appearances and relativisation); on the other, the Heracliteans are ostensibly historical personages, and Cratylus is certainly not represented as merely a character in a Platonic dialogue (not that we can be sure that Aristotle is concerned to mark such distinctions). But Aristotle is after the philosophical truth, and feels he has secured the dialectical high ground. Of course these fellows insisted on total change; but we know (because we have arguments to that effect) that change is not omnipresent – just as we know that knowledge is not to be defined as perception – and are free to use true propositions against them, regardless of whether they were ignorant of them, or would resist their adoption if informed. For Aristotle, the *raison d'être* of doxography is the confirmation of the (Aristotelian) truth by finding reassuring anticipations of his doctrines in his predecessors, clearing away potentially distracting alternatives, and donning the gauntlets when necessary. To some scholars, this makes him an unreliable and unscrupulous 'historian' at best, always working from his distorting agenda, foxing us with harmful parodies of all and sundry. Even the most pious Aristotelian must admit discomfort at some of Aristotle's quick and sneaky doxographical moves; but, when he is on form, his engagement with and transformation of the history of philosophy are unsurpassed. Plato showed us Socrates in ventriloquistic discussion *with* Protagoras. Aristotle teaches us how to talk *about* Cratylus. Not with him.

Were he for real, he not only read Heraclitus as an advocate of radical flux, but also drew the conclusion that whereof one cannot speak, thereof one must keep silent; presumably the finger moves not to point at this or that, which has already changed by the time you follow the gesture, but rather by waving about ceaselessly to indicate that there is nothing to indicate.[19] If you have been won over by Aristotle, you won't speak to the wagging finger, but rather shake your head in resignation and walk on by.

Chapter 3

A life without belief?

In conclusion we jump far forward in history, to the (post-) Hellenistic Sceptics. There is both continuity with and expansion of what has gone before. Since Sceptics claim to be commitment-free, they are neither Heracliteans nor Protagoreans (although, as we shall see, our longstanding dialectical partners will not altogether disappear from the scene); but, like our Presocratic and Sophist (or like their Platonic and Aristotelian traditional representations), they do adopt a posture which the opposition declares indefensible. The Sceptical strategy is to deny that defence is required, since, in a manner to be explained, there is nothing there to attack: not since, like Cratylus, they have renounced language (to a Sceptic, he is no better off than the articulate exponent of any other dogmatic theory), but rather because they feel able to do dialectic without themselves getting trammelled in unreliable and unsettling conviction. Moreover, this active intellectual and emotional freedom is *lived*, not just an 'academic' stance playfully adopted within the parlour of philosophy.

Pyrrho ' . . . seems to have practised philosophy in a most noble way, introducing that form of it which consists in non-cognition and suspension of judgement . . . For he would maintain that nothing is honourable or base, or just or unjust, and that likewise in all cases nothing exists in truth; and that convention and habit are the basis of everything that men do; for each thing is no more this than this. He followed these principles in his actual way of life, avoiding nothing and taking no precautions, facing everything as it came, wagons, precipices, dogs, and entrusting nothing whatsoever to his sensations. But he was looked after, as Antigonus of Carystus reports, by his disciples who accompanied him. Aenesidemus, however, says that although he practised philosophy on the principles of suspension of judgement, he did not act carelessly in the details of daily life. He lived to be nearly ninety' (LS [= Long and Sedley 1987] 1A.2 – 4). Like Socrates, although of a later generation – Pyrrho was Aristotle's younger contemporary – he was a figure who, despite writing nothing, was to inspire a philosophical movement ('Pyrrhonism'); and, again like Socrates, the inspiration seems to have stemmed not only from what he might have said, but also, and much more, from the example of his life as an enactment of philosophy. This life was so impressive that it attracted the respectful interest even of those who had no truck with his ideas: Nausiphanes 'used to say, at any rate, that it was Pyrrho's character one needed to get but his own doctrines; and he would frequently say that Epicurus also admired Pyrrho's lifestyle and was always asking him about Pyrrho' (LS 1B.2). And what was so deeply impressive? That would depend on which strand of the doxography one traces. 'When he [Pyrrho] was once scared by a dog that set on him, he responded to criticism by saying that it was difficult to strip oneself completely of being human . . . ' (LS 1C.1). That sounds like the Pyrrho of Antigonus; he is admirable for his extreme and extraordinary effort at self-transformation, in accordance with his principles. 'He was always in the same mental state' (LS 1B.1); and that state was one of complete and impregnable tranquillity (consult the useful texts in LS 2). Claims for the blessedness of Pyrrho's existence are plentiful in the tradition of Aenesidemus, which denies that inner tranquillity was buffered by the efforts of busy carers.

And, once more, the doxography presents us with a problem, the Pyrrhonian Question. What are 'non-cognition and suspension of judgement'? Evidently lack of opinion, a refusal to commit oneself; but about what, and on what grounds? 'Nothing' suggests about everything (although the examples are of moral predicates); and perhaps 'each thing is no more this than this' and the invocation of 'convention and habit' suggest that Pyrrho's reaction to conflicting appearances was not relativistic,[1] but rather the nihilistic conclusion that 'nothing exists in truth'. And how would one live, were that one's conclusion? This is the Question. According to Aenesidemus, Pyrrho was no reckless maniac (and he did reach a ripe old age): but, in that case, did he really 'practise philosophy on the principles of suspension of judgement'? Surely, you might think, one would take prudent precautions only if one *believed* that dangers are to be avoided? According to Antigonus, Pyrrho's adherence to his principles was straightforward, so that he was in constant need of minders. But in that case, although you might admire his (insanely?) brave consistency, you might well doubt that such a life is really liveable, requiring as it does protection and rescue from responsible others. And if some disciple must pull Pyrrho away from the cliff's edge, surely that disciple believes that in truth it is better not to topple over? Were that so, the minders who follow Pyrrho about ironically cannot themselves follow his principles; and a philosophy sincere adherence to which demands that others do *not* 'suspend judgement' would seem to be parasitic on supposedly false commitment, a most unattractive situation.

As with Socrates, our concern is not to answer the historical Question. The scant evidence for Pyrrho does indeed indicate that he maintained that 'nothing exists *in truth*', 'each thing *is* no more this than this' (we can only conjecture about the arguments he adduced). What we shall focus on is the *status* of such disclaimers: is it *true* that 'nothing exists in truth'? What of the 'thing', that 'each thing is no more this than this': is that, too, a matter of indifference? The Introduction gave you an example of how to trap Sceptics who give the wrong, dogmatic answers to these questions, tripping them into self-refutation. Some thinkers in, or associated with, Pyrrho's tradition sought to avoid the trap (e.g. the saying that 'we know nothing, nor do we even know just this, that we know nothing' [LS 1D] is attributed to Metrodorus): but what, then, do the Sceptics have to go on, how might they participate in dialectic, knowing nothing? We shall see that they pretend to possess a much more remarkable, iconoclastic ability: to get by without belief, let alone knowledge. That concerns the viability of the *philosophical* life for the Sceptic. According to Antigonus, Pyrrho 'entrusted nothing whatsoever to his sensations'. But Timon, Pyrrho's most important disciple, declares: 'that honey is sweet I do not affirm, but I agree that it appears so' (LS 1H.3). The Protagoras of the *Theaetetus* maintains that what appears to X is true-for-X: can a Sceptic get by not with relativised truth, but rather on the basis of the appearances alone, reacting to their suggestions without endorsing them as true reports about reality ('it seems to me there's a precipice in front of me, which I feel like avoiding' – and he turns away)? That concerns the viability of the philosophical *life* for the Sceptic.

The key to understanding sophisticated Sceptical strategies is to be found in their methodology. 'Non-cognition and suspension of judgement', which we have not glossed so far, must be given a sense which on the one hand acquits them of dogmatic inconsistency, on the other does not disable them from surviving the tribulations of daily life and engaging in dialectic with other philosophers. Aenesidemus, who lived in the first century BC, broke away from the Academy which, he felt, had lapsed into dogmatism,[2] to found the radical Pyrrhonian movement. In a report of his *Pyrrhonist Discourses*, we read that members of his school ' . . . are aporetic and free of all doctrine. Not one of them has said either that all things are incognitive, or that they are cognitive, but that they are no more of this kind than of that . . . Nor indeed, do they say there is true or false, convincing or unconvincing, existent or non-existent. But the same thing is, it might be said, no more true than false, convincing than unconvincing, or existent than non-existent; or sometimes the one, sometimes the other; or of such a kind for one person but not for another. For the Pyrrhonist determines absolutely nothing, not even this very claim that nothing is determined. (We put it this way, he says, for lack of a way to express the thought)' (LS 71C.6 – 8). Why all that variation in the formulation of what Pyrrhonism does (or doesn't?) stand for? Precisely in order to avoid the dogmatic horn of the dilemma: for 'each thing *is* no more this than this', we substitute 'they *are no more* of this kind than of that' (and is that itself true?). They say neither that 'there is true or false' – nor, by the same token, do they deny it. But if the Pyrrhonists are genuinely aporetic, what do they have to say to other philosophers? The end of the quotation seems to be an admission that the Sceptics are in expressive difficulties – if they are so fettered, how are they to cope with the dogmatic threat?

Simply to opt out of dialectic is to relinquish any claim to be a philosopher, by Greek standards; the secret is to take advantage of the dialectic that has already happened or is happening, rather than to initiate it. 'Whether it is or is not such as it appears he [Pyrrho][3] does not assert, because he thinks that the arguments for the opposing views are of equal strength, and he makes the impressions on a par with each other . . . ' (LS 71D.3).[4] As I said in the Introduction, the Sceptic is a Searcher or Investigator. Amongst the conflicting appearances, by this mature stage in the history of Greek philosophy, are to be found a great many competing theories on every conceivable philosophical topic. One impartially discovers that when opposing arguments are placed in the balance of reason, they turn out to be of equal weight, so that the only rational thing to do is to suspend judgement – and thus free oneself of intellectual disturbance, and concomitant emotional turbulence. But what if the argumentative scales don't balance out? 'He *makes*': the ingenious Sceptic does more history of philosophy, so as to increase the quantity of opinion on the lighter side,[5] and might also invent novel arguments, not *in propria persona* but *ad hominem*, so as to increase their quality.[6] What standards of validity are applicable? Whatever regulates the dialectic of those dogmatists, especially the Stoics, who think they know what makes for a logically persuasive argument; with the consequence that so far from being disabled, the Sceptics can say to their opponents 'if faithful to your own principles, you too ought to join our camp'. Note that the Sceptic is no Protagorean, for whom alternative positions, all true, are not really in competition.[7] That appearances conflict means they cannot all be true; but, no matter which dogmatic criterion of truth is invoked, there is no winner. The proper response is not to deny that truth exists, with the historical Pyrrho: maybe it does not; or maybe it remains latent within the appearances, beyond our ken until now. Of course, one doesn't stop: since Sceptics don't assert that it is true that all opposing arguments are equal, they keep on investigating (discovering, to their imperturbable delight,[8] that it keeps on seeming that way); and there is always another dogmatist to liberate. It turns out that so far from being a non-starter, Scepticism properly undertaken is *the* philosophical life.

So much for how to avoid both renouncing dialectic and self-refutation on the basis of dogmatic commitment; what about quotidian existence? 'Nor was suspension of judgement about everything disturbed by those who toiled away and wrote lengthy arguments against it. But having finally confronted it from the Stoa with "inactivity" like a Gorgon, they faded away, since for all their twisting and turning, impulse refused to become assent, and did not accept sensation as tipping the balance, but was seen to lead to action on its own initiative without needing assent . . . The movement of impression we could not remove, even if we wanted to; rather, as soon as we encounter things, we get an impression and are affected by them . . . So whenever something appropriate has appeared, no opinion is needed to get us moving and proceeding towards it . . . "But how is it that someone who suspends judgement does not rush away to a mountain instead of to the bath, or out to the market-place?" . . . Because, of course, it is not the mountain but the bath that appears a bath to him, not the wall but the door that appears a door, and likewise with everything else' (LS 69A.1 – 6). This is from Plutarch, on behalf of the Academy; but the Pyrrhonists happily took over this defensive strategy, which is also to be found in Sextus Empiricus (e.g. in his work *Adversus Mathematicos* XI 162 – 3). In Greek mythology, the Gorgon petrified those unfortunates who gazed on her face; thus the Stoics, the arch dogmatic enemies of the non-doctrinal Academy, argued that one who really suspends judgement must, in consistency, lapse into total inactivity. Why? Stoic philosophy of action teaches that when we receive sensory impressions, we react accordingly to their input; but the reactive impulses which issue in action occur only once we have evaluated these impressions for truth; an impulse is a reaction to an impression to which we have assented. No assent, no impulse; no impulse, no action; since assent is assent to truth, one who suspends judgement should be frozen to the spot. The dialectical counter-move is to remove assent from the equation: my irrational, unmeditated and instinctual reaction suffices for me to snatch my hand away from the fire, to eat bread rather than coal, without my committing myself to 'fire really *is* hot, burns really *are* bad' or 'bread *truly* is nutritious, coal isn't'.[9] And, to all appearances, Sceptics will lead normal lives, subscribing to social conventions, since Sextus teaches that they also react non-committally to ordinary cultural input – they go with the flow. But, despite these appearances, the Sceptic is not at all the same as his benighted fellow citizen or co-worker, since he doesn't *believe* any of it.

So are the Sceptics off the hook, proponents of a tenable, indeed attractive and exciting philosophical approach? Remember that in the Introduction I said that it would, of course, be crazy to aspire actually to become an ancient Greek philosopher – might that have been too precipitate? For sure a modern true believer in Aristotelian natural philosophy or psychology would be worse than eccentric; but if the Sceptical life is the life *without* belief, why shouldn't it remain liveable, since one would be shedding our modern doxastic baggage, not acquiring any additional antique commitments? If anything, you might think that we could function as more effective Sceptics than the ancients. The range of issues on which to suspend judgement has grown (is there an external world? How can I know that I'm not a brain in a vat, subjected to illusory stimulation by mad scientists?); and the stock of conflicting arguments has increased explosively, just as Sextus predicted (see note 6), so that there is very much more ammunition to load into the Sceptical modes than the Greeks ever dreamt of (see note 5). Contemporary scepticism is a challenge, not to belief as such, which it leaves intact, but rather to the possibility of knowledge, querying whether we can ever satisfy one or another criterion for knowledge, or, if so, whether we can know that we know; and such epistemological arguments typically take the form of the construction and analysis of elaborate thought experiments by philosophers who do not themselves venture to advocate scepticism. Thus the appearance of a new Pyrrhonist would certainly affect the philosophical scene in a big way. If original Scepticism is tranquil adherence to a liberated and liberating philosophical method, rather than to any set of antique dogmas, why not become a convert and keep the tradition of Greek philosophy alive by casting in one's lot with them?

Thinking that one over will be our final task. And you know by now not to expect me to dissipate the *aporia*. Let us take it case by case. First, sense impressions. Here the Sceptics seem to have solid ground beneath their feet. When my stomach is empty, I feel hungry; if I fill it with decent food, that feels good, and I spit out garbage without hesitation, unthinkingly. What helps with the denial that assent to the truth of these impressions need intervene is the fact that infants and irrational animals do the same sort of thing. Admittedly, only a few of my reactions to sensory stimuli are as unmediated as pure reflexes; but it is not so implausible to contend that my conscious apprehension of and reaction to the environment might rely on unendorsed appearances, recorded in 'it seems to me that . . . ' formulae.

Second, the rational impressions with which language-users are bombarded by their cultural *milieu*. Here the ground is not so promisingly firm. Suppose I am a doctor (Sextus himself may or may not have been one). To a non-Sceptic, I will appear a play-actor. I say things like 'the blood circulates, pumped about the body by the heart; diabetics require insulin; surgical instruments must be carefully sterilised . . . '; but, if pressed, I shrug my shoulders and confess that the blood no more circulates than it doesn't, etc.[10] The only reason I diagnose and treat cardiac complaints as I do is that current orthodoxy so dictates, and I'm a professional conformist. Although perhaps many of us dogmatic patients won't be reassured, the Sceptic is not in immediate trouble: after all, if the play-acting is perfect, if the non-believing doctor will behave just as a dogmatic counterpart would, the treatment will be identical, and our chances of being cured remain the same. But what if I have cancer and go in for a consultation to hear this? 'I'm afraid there are several competing potential cures, and the jury is out; I prescribe this one, because . . . ' 'Because' what, exactly? The consistently Sceptical practitioner replies: 'I've read the medical journals conscientiously, and consulted my expert colleagues. Let's go for treatment C, because . . . '. Now what must not be said is ' . . . because the balance of probabilities suggests that C is more likely to have captured the true aetiology of your disease, and thus to have prescribed something which will really work'. Instead, the doctor must say: 'because my educated hunch is that C appears to be more likely than not to become orthodoxy – because it will *seem* efficacious'.[11]

At this point you might be nervously wondering how it is that some remedies work, others don't. Your desire is not (only) to feel healthy, but to be in a state of health, since a specious appearance will lead, sooner or later, to feeling painfully unhealthy. Dogmatic doctors account for orthodoxy by reference to the truth about the body, and how to cure it (of course if they are not excessively 'dogmatic' in the pejorative, non-philosophical sense of the word, they hedge their bets on the veracity of some of the current orthodoxy). Sceptical doctors can only appeal to a pragmatic criterion for their policies; and it is far from clear that that suffices. Invoking the modes, one notices that there are homeopaths and other assorted quacks eager to prescribe treatments which the orthodox condemn as at best useless, at worst positively harmful: why isn't the Sceptical doctor NHS one day for me, a reflexologist or faith healer tomorrow for you?

The crunch comes with the third case, the Sceptic's claim to engage in dialectic without thereby getting entangled in doxastic commitments. Sextus famously likens Pyrrhonism to an emetic which purges itself together with the poisonous dogmas, or a ladder which once scaled into the tranquil heights should be cast aside (*Adversus Mathematicos* VIII 481): but is it really possible to use all his dialectical equipment, and then put it away with clean hands? Your first thought might be that this should prove much easier than the second case. After all, there is no ruling philosophical orthodoxy corresponding to the medical one, reputable philosophers remain at perennial loggerheads, so that recourse to the modes does not seem bizarre and dangerous. OK, it's not clear that I can operate successfully as a Sceptical doctor. But my aspirations are philosophical; why not immerse myself in all the traditions, Greek and others, and live as a professional Sceptical philosopher?

We come to the nub of the matter. The Sceptic says: 'I have read some Plato, which argues for the immortality of the soul; and some Epicurus, which argues *contra*. And these arguments balance out (before my intervention, Epicurus seemed to have the better of the argument, but I niftily tweaked the *Phaedo* to add just enough weight on that side). So I suspend judgement on the fate of the soul (if there is one)'. But recollect how one evaluates arguments – in terms of validity and soundness. Never mind about soundness; the problem for the Sceptic is not whether the arguments might be as good as all that. A valid argument, remember, is one whose premises necessitate the truth of its conclusion: how is the Sceptic to evaluate validity, without having recourse to the concept of truth? Is he not saying, 'it seems to me as likely that were the *Phaedo*'s premises true, immortality would follow, as that the truth of Epicurus' conclusion follows necessarily from his premises'? In the schema 'X seems p to me', if I fill it in to get 'honey seems sweet to me', nothing stops me from adding 'but I suspend judgement on whether it is true that honey is sweet'. But if I want to reach the pro tem conclusion that some arguments balance out, 'they seem equally persuasive to me', other philosophers will take me seriously only if I explain why they seem equally persuasive; and that I can do only by stating that they strike me as equally (likely to be) (in)valid, where validity inevitably brings in truth. If that is so, then you cannot emulate the Sceptics: they must either drop out of the philosophical game or admit defeat on the score of self-refutation.[12]

This is not the last word. You might feel that the evasive *ad hominem* strategy, which should be applied not only to substantive doctrine but also to formal dialectical procedure, has not been exploited to the full. Could the Sceptic not invite the dogmatist to explicate validity by his lights, and 'demonstrate' equality playing strictly by the other's rules? There would be no need to make any commitment to their authenticity; and one might pick up different sets of logical procedures in tune with the various tastes of the opponent, only to cast them aside when off dialectical duty. In fact Sextus shows that the Sceptics did very cleverly attempt to turn Stoic logic against its inventors. But the problem would remain that the life of a Sceptic involves more than polemical exchanges, defensive and offensive; they also investigate off their own bat, always finding themselves poised in pleasant indecision, since the rational course is to suspend judgement. During these independent episodes, what logical criteria are available for safe employment? Were the Sceptic to give up autonomous philosophising to avoid dogmatism and be restricted to reactive dialectic, that life loses much of its attractions, because so parasitic: if Antigonus' Pyrrho required friendly minders to survive in body, so we shall depend on the availability of hostile material to survive in mind (and even then we could only ask 'don't the arguments seem of equal weight to you?', without saying that they seem that way to us). But the Sceptics have a final trick up their sleeves. Some of them astoundingly conceded self-refutation, but refused thereby to

123

concede the game – they argued that self-refutation was grist to their mill, since it helpfully eliminates the Sceptical purgative, leaving the mind cleansed of all contaminating commitments (e.g. *Outlines of Pyrrhonism* I 14 – 15).[13] Could this possibly be so? Digest the arguments. If persuaded – according to which logical canons? – I look forward to meeting a live Sceptic (although I am not sure that you will have much to say for yourself). If not convinced that validity can be coherently uncoupled from truth, you will bracket the Sceptics with the contradictory Heracliteans (or maybe you have arguments to rescue them?); there is no tenable position in conceptual space for them to occupy. But you will probably agree that it is good to do philosophy about and with them.

Notes

Introduction: doing and living philosophy

1   Here I am mimicking Aristotle, who in his early piece the *Protrepticus* (an exhortation to turn to philosophy; a great many works in this genre were composed, and so entitled) makes almost exactly the same move. Approximately: 'if you should philosophise, you should philosophise; if you shouldn't philosophise, to arrive at that view you are already philosophising'.

2   As I said, very roughly put (to be more precise, its real form is: 'there is exactly one girl in the next room, and there is no girl in the next room who does not have red hair'; and since the first component of this statement is false, so is the entire statement). When the subject of a sentence is a description which fails to refer, such as 'the girl in the next room', is that sentence false, or rather neither true nor false, given the failure of reference? Modern logicians argue the pros and cons of these competing analyses.

3   For virtue ethics, consult the essays in Crisp and Slote 1997.

4   Hilary Putnam is one of the original functionalists, Martha Nussbaum the functionalist Aristotelian; Myles Burnyeat is their opponent. See the series of chapters on philosophy of mind in Putnam 1975, especially 'The Nature of Mental States', to learn more; Burnyeat 1995 for the challenge he mounts; and Nussbaum and Putnam 1995 for their defence. This is very advanced stuff, and assumes a background in both philosophy and Aristotle, but if you can penetrate the arguments, they will impart suggestive lessons about what is at stake in the history of philosophy.

5   This is only to scratch the surface. (3) 'If you are a century old, you are reading this book; you are a century old; so you are reading this book.' (4) 'If you are less than a century old, you are not reading this book; you are less than a century old; so you are not reading this book.' What to make of these arguments? Well, inasmuch as you are reading this book, (3) looks better than (4); on the other hand, inasmuch as you're not that old, (4) looks better than (3) – but what does your age have to do with what you're currently up to? We sense that for Y to follow from X, they must be properly connected; Y must be true *because* X is true. Many brilliant logicians from Aristotle to the present day have contributed to the solution of this problem; it is not yet solved, completely and to everyone's satisfaction.

6   This is cautious: there are indeed some Latin patristic writers who rely almost entirely on Latin sources, and I am not confident that some pagan philosophers did not follow suit (although I cannot think of any). But better to err on the side of caution, since in any case these Latins are in a tiny minority.

7   Long's chapter on Roman philosophy in Sedley 2003 is a good map for those who wish to enter this terrain.

8   Lloyd 1996 is a nuanced comparative study of ancient Greek and Chinese philosophy and science, highly recommended because it concentrates on methodologies, styles of thought, and institutional and social frameworks.

9   Some *caveats* should be entered, but the qualifications are minor. For example, it has long been assumed that since the Hellenistic philosophers came after Aristotle, and he is a philosopher of such

genius, they must have been strongly influenced by his work. But Harry Sandbach mounted a sceptical case against any Aristotelian influence on the Stoics, one of the greatest of the Hellenistic schools (Sandbach 1985). Some scholars dismiss Sandbach's thesis in its entirety, others accept only a sub-set of his results; but it is reasonable to conclude that the Greek tradition, remarkable unity that it is, has gaps and discontinuities. Nevertheless, one has only to read, for example, Simplicius, a philosopher who lived in the sixth century AD and wrote commentaries on Aristotle, to verify that this was a living and continuous movement stretching back for a millennium. Later in this book I shall have much more to say about how Greek reflection on the philosophical past simultaneously discovered a tradition that was already there, and also helped to create it.

10 Guthrie 1962 – 81 is the fullest English language history of Greek philosophy, and the standard work of its type. Some of it is out of date, and Guthrie is not very acute philosophically; but he does not skirt the arguments and is excellent for basic orientation. Since he only goes up to Aristotle, you can use Long and Sedley 1987 for the Hellenistic philosophers (Long and Sedley are exceptionally acute and provide much more than orientation, but are also very accessible as a way in). Sedley 2003 is a very useful work by many hands, arranged chronologically, and includes chapters on the interaction between philosophy, religion and science, and on the later influence of ancient philosophy. It would be a good idea to use these and other books I shall recommend in conjunction with this one, to gain a fuller picture. The absence of scholarship not written in English arises from my target audience and is not a reflection on the quality of non-Anglophone research.

11 The books of Aristotle's *Metaphysics* are labelled by the letters of the Greek alphabet, of which *gamma* is the third letter (and names the fourth book, since there are two books lettered 'alpha', 'big' and 'little').

12 My generalisation does not imply unanimity: agreement over the significance of philosophy co-exists with the sharpest disagreement over what philosophy is, and how its life is to be lived. Ancient

Cynicism is a case in point. As with 'scepticism / Scepticism', so here common usage is potentially misleading. We think of a 'cynic' as a possibly embittered rejector of something or other. I might be cynical about a politician's promises. I don't trust him, or politicians in general; and, depending on my estimation of politics, my cynical attitude might range from mildly scoffing to fiercely outraged. You might be a cynical person *tout court*, morose, sarcastic, misanthropic, trusting no one and detecting cant and hypocrisy everywhere. Capital 'C' Cynics were an ancient movement, whose adherents despised conventional morality and engaged in deliberately outrageous behaviour (e.g. masturbating in public) which supposedly cleaved to 'nature'. Were the Cynics philosophers? The answer is unclear. No one who abjures the responsibilities of argument is a philosopher; and many Cynics seem to have operated more as inflammatory performance artists, as it were, rather than in the guise of arguers. On the other hand, there was an easily recognisable Cynic way of life, and they had a decided influence on the Stoics, some of whom combined allegiance to certain Cynic attitudes with full engagement in dialectic.

13　It is often said that 'happiness' is a bad translation of *eudaimonia*, because the connotations of the English word are misleading. It is true that when used in phrases such as 'I feel happy' or 'she has a happy disposition', to refer either to a transient mood or cheerful outlook, 'happiness' vocabulary is inappropriate for *eudaimonia*. This is because, in such usages, the connotations of the English are subjective, characterising one's occurrent emotions and emotional attitudes. The problem is that while *eudaimonia* does involve feelings, they must be the *right* feelings; and it includes much more than feelings, since it is an objective condition. A happy mood can be short-lived and an unusual person might feel happy in adverse circumstances, but *eudaimonia* is neither temporary nor compatible with failure, where doing well or ill is judged from a third-person perspective. This is all true, but in other usages – e.g. 'she succeeded in living a happy life', 'he finally achieved happiness' – the semantics are not so divergent. In any case, Aristotelian *eudaimonia* is a notion which develops from the conceptual repertoire of native Greek speakers, but is subjected to philosophical analysis which takes it far beyond common understanding. If one bears this in mind, 'happiness' doesn't hurt.

14 You might use Broadie and Rowe 2002 for this independent study.

1 Opposition, relativism, contradiction

1 Nightingale 1995 is very good on Plato's project of self-demarcation.

2 If you have read some Platonic dialogues, you might feel unhappy with my list, even as a partial catalogue. In some dialogues, Socrates espouses theories of dialectic which are not question-and-answer, and recommends alternative and often recondite definitional techniques (e.g. the *Phaedrus*, the *Sophist*, the *Philebus*); Plato portrays him expounding and defending a doctrine of incorporeal, changeless, absolute and transcendent entities, the so-called 'Forms' (e.g. the *Phaedo*, the *Republic*); in some dialogues the *definienda* are not ethical items – although finding their definitions is still supposed to be of tremendous ethical import (e.g. the *Theaetetus* itself, our primary Platonic text); sometimes Socrates advocates a psychology which denies that knowledge of what is good guarantees its performance (e.g. the *Republic*). Quite so. Scholars concur that what Plato attributes to Socrates is very diverse; they disagree over whether it is all compatible, and over how much of it Plato intended us to assign to Socrates, rather than himself. 'The Socratic Question' asks: who was the real, historical Socrates? (Vlastos 1991 is a classic attempt to answer the question.) Some Platonic scholars ('developmentalists') believe that Plato's philosophy evolved radically over time, and segregate a group of supposedly early dialogues which, they think, represent (something like) the historical Socrates. None of the cited dialogues, with the exception of the *Theaetetus*, ever appears within this group; and some developmentalists adduce Aristotle's concurrence with the representation of Socrates in the 'early' group as evidence for their thesis. Disagreement over the Socratic Question still rages; and

allegiance to developmentalism is not responsible for my catalogue. As I stated in the Introduction, we are looking into how the Greek philosophical tradition created itself; for that purpose, it is those aspects of the Platonic and Aristotelian picture of Socrates which came to distinguish him from the Presocratics which are relevant, regardless of whatever narrowly historical (viz factual) inaccuracies they might mask.

3   Chronology is not the heart of the matter. The lives of some Presocratics (e.g. Democritus) overlapped with Socrates'; but the classification is unaffected, since the likes of Democritus were uninfluenced by Socratic innovations.

4   The bible of Presocratic studies: henceforth, as is conventional, I shall refer to this book as KRS, and identify fragments and *testimonia* by KRS number.

5   Translations of the Presocratics are adaptations of those in KRS.

6   Compare 'I want that toad in the hole': how would you analyse this sentence's ambiguity?

7   A possible objection: the literary culture of Heraclitus' day is generally thought to have been oral in character; an ambiguity in the written script is not at all necessarily one that carries through to the oral delivery, and in this particular case it might be quite hard to retain it in speaking. (Cf.: were I to blurt out 'Jack-is-fine-and-Jill-is-wretched' all in one breath, you get the ambiguity in my example; but maybe if I pause after uttering the first clause, you might incline to viewing me as an unambiguous enemy of Jill's.) Hard, but not impossible. Perhaps more important: one might speculate that Heraclitus' obsession with oracular hermeneutics – on which more below – might well have induced him deliberately to cultivate the indeterminacy of script (and Greek writing of this period was entirely unpunctuated, indeed the words were undivided) where oral delivery would clarify (an ingenious or perverse preference, depending on one's philosophical taste).

8   Kahn 1979 is an illuminating monograph which is exceptionally helpful with Heraclitus' language, whether or not you know Greek.

9   On the other hand, one might counter that 'I searched out . . . ' need not imply ' . . . and *found* myself', or even go so far as to con-

tend that Heraclitus' assertion that it is impossible to reach the limits of the soul ('you would not find out the boundaries of soul, even by travelling along every path: so deep a measure does it have' [KRS 232]) positively militates against reading KRS 246 as advertising his success in auto-psychoanalysis. In any event, the solution I propose holds good however one interprets KRS 246.

10   I should point out that some scholars go for a minimalist reading of Heraclitean *logos*, according to which it has no more than its semantic core of speech or language; *logos* in its extended senses is supposed to be incorrectly read back into Heraclitus from its later employment by the Stoics, who spoke of *logos* as cosmic principle. I think this minimalism cannot be right, since it makes it impossible to understand how we are to move from Heraclitus' *logos* in the sense of what he *says* to the common *logos* in the sense of the way the world *is*.

11   Radical environmentalists and animal rights activists, of course, are exceptions to this generalisation: they certainly do take the attitudes and interests of non-human animals very seriously. However, the most common type of plea used by such movements works by arguing from what we *share* with the other animals. For example, it might be claimed that it is wrong to inflict painful suffering on innocent sentient beings, that therefore animals should not be slaughtered for food, and we should be vegetarians. When such pleas are entertained, debate usually centres on whether there really is a single experience of moral significance shared by us and other species. For example, an opponent of vegetarianism might argue that the kind of pain humans suffer is so different from animal pain that it is illegitimate to argue that animal suffering is morally significant (or significant in the way and to the extent that human suffering is). Or take fish-eating 'vegetarians': they believe that there is morally significant pain suffered by humans and some animals, but that the nervous system of fish is incapable of experiencing it (others disagree). My point is that it is a given in such arguments that they turn on attempts to assimilate other species to ours; contrast Heraclitus, who seizes on difference, and makes no attempt to reduce heterogeneity. It is worth pondering these

diametrically opposed ways of situating human beings *vis-à-vis* other animals.

12 The connections might well be historical, as well as thematic; as Malcolm Schofield remarks, 'in some ways Heraclitus looks like nothing so much as Xenophanes' most attentive pupil . . . ' (from his chapter on the Presocratics, Sedley 2003: 57).

13 You might know that one of the charges brought against Socrates in the trial which led to his execution was impiety, 'the introduction of new gods': doesn't this show that Athenian religion was doxastic? In fact the reverse. In the *Apology* of Plato, Socrates spends most of his time rebutting the other charge, that he corrupted the youth of the city, and deals with impiety relatively briefly. He counters that his fellow-citizens have all seen him in attendance at public festivals; that is, he cites what he did, not what he claims to believe. Were belief as such paramount, Socrates would have been vulnerable to the riposte 'ah – but what unorthodox thoughts were going through your mind?'. One might object: 'but he *was* vulnerable to that riposte; the reason for his pointing to his conduct is that it constitutes publicly available *evidence* for his beliefs. Had he simply cited his beliefs, that would not have carried any weight in court'. Answer: although the ancient Greek concepts of legal testimony, evidence, etc., differ strikingly from ours, and their practice of prosecution and defence correspondingly diverges from ours, we and they share a sharp nose for protestations wide open to accusations of hypocrisy; and nothing is an easier target than 'I went through the motions'. The *Apology* is not a transcript of what Socrates said. However, ancient Athenian defendants – who could not avail themselves of the services of a representative – might nevertheless commission a skilled speech writer, who would provide a script for anything from rote memorisation, in the case of a dullard, to an improvisatory template, in the case of an intelligent client. Certainly the Platonic portrait of Socrates excludes his needing a borrowed voice: the *Apology* purports to be what he said off his own bat, either *ex tempore* or on the basis of his rhetorical repertoire. But in any case, Plato would not depict Socrates, in this context, as committing so egregious a forensic blunder as simply

gesturing at his actions, given the obvious slip between (empty) deeds and hidden thoughts. True, the *Apology* bristles with deliberate bolshiness – most obviously, Socrates' recommendation that he be 'penalised' by civic honours – but he is never shown to be cackhanded in this arena.

14 If the Greeks lacked canonical scriptures, why imagine my hypothetical conservative turning to Homer and Hesiod? Why couldn't he say: 'well, Xenophanes, I concede that these poems are chock full of scandalous myths; but they're just blasphemous drivel'? If not scriptural, these texts were nevertheless held in the highest esteem; and anyway, non-literary religious accounts were every bit as susceptible to Xenophanes' critique.

15 Yes and no. In many ways, they – especially Homer – are 'like' the Bible (at least until the last few decades): venerability, total familiarity, availability for anything from superficial, even flip, citation to learned and earnest exegesis, etc. But even if divine words through the inspirational conduit of the muses, the foundational epics are not God's words, to be accorded unqualified respect with the threat of institutionalised penalty for blasphemous disrespect. The contrast with the Bible holds good, for both literalists and allegorists (allegorisation was a thriving trade for Greek intellectuals, since, by their lights, it was the way to reconcile the cultural prestige of Homer and Hesiod with whatever their favoured philosophy might be).

16 'Asses prefer garbage to gold' (not in KRS; Kahn 1979 fr. 71); 'swine delight in mire more than clear water; chickens bathe in dust' (Kahn fr. 72). These may not be *verbatim* quotations, but must be very close to the Heraclitean originals.

17 Cf. Heraclitus: 'the most beautiful of apes is ugly in comparison with the race of man; the wisest of men seems an ape in comparison to a god' (Kahn fr. 56). This is not so far away from Xenophanes' thought experiment (although of course the train of thought is not the same). It is a very elegant and clever example of the unity of opposites. 'Man is beautiful (compared to an ape); and not . . . .' Now you expect ' . . . not beautiful (compared to an . . .)'; but instead you get 'foolish in comparison to a god', shifting the

standard from beauty to wisdom so as to conjoin three terms, animal, human, god, by means of two criteria, looks and intelligence.

18 The Greek word is *harmonia*; although not nearly as restricted as the etymological descendant 'harmony', it has inescapable musical connotations, especially given the reference to the lyre. One should have 'attunement' (in both literal and metaphorical senses) at the back of one's mind, when thinking about Heraclitus' 'connection'.

19 'There comes' as such isn't in the Greek, but this does not affect my point.

20 Such a theory is sketched in Plato's very Heraclitean dialogue the *Symposium*.

21 This is the interpretation endorsed by KRS; Kahn 1979 contains an extended and thoughtful version. For a spirited defence of the ascription of 'everything flows' to the historical Heraclitus, see Barnes 1982 (this book comes very highly recommended for the quality of its argumentative engagement with all the Presocratic philosophers). All these writers are scholarly philosophers, experts in the field, but have reached opposing verdicts on Heraclitean change. You can make up your mind only by testing their arguments against the evidence; that is, by doing Greek philosophy.

22 To be perfectly accurate: for Aristotle, Heraclitus himself is in the dock; for Plato (always a more *louche*, and perhaps, curiously enough, a fairer and more generous doxographer) the 'Heracliteans'.

23 The Introduction discussed Greek philosophy's bid for privileged authority through the claim that it seeks wisdom by argument. Heraclitus' advancement of the *logos* before himself is an example of this. Its paradoxical difficulty – can we really heed the *logos*, *rather than* Heraclitus himself? – is paralleled by Parmenides' dialectical strategy. On the one hand, Parmenides' conception of reality is expounded by means of a sustained logical deduction, argument in its purest form. On the other, for his exposition he adopts all the trappings of the religious and literary tradition, pretending that his *logos* came from the mouth of a goddess: divine revelation or argument? If divine revelation, isn't Parmenides illicitly taking advantage of irrational paraphernalia to insinuate that his

doctrine enjoys an authority not stemming from argument and nothing but argument? This is a nice question; since the goddess exhorts Parmenides to attend to her words, one might venture the guess that he, rather like Heraclitus, is in fact encouraging us ultimately to respect what is said, not the speaker – even a divine one. But it is hard not to suspect that Parmenides is trying to have it both ways. Thus we see that from its Presocratic beginnings Greek philosophers were extremely sensitive to methodological issues. And Parmenides' dilemma remains unresolved: to this day those hostile to philosophy accuse it of duplicity (for example, 'Plato was the greatest rhetorician of all in his condemnation of rhetoric'). You can learn more about these debates from Wardy 1996.

2 Refuting the irrefutable?

1 To be precise, according to the Stoics, only bodies can cause; but *what* they cause can be immaterial predicates – e.g. the sun (a body) causes the wax to melt (viz makes a new predicate apply to the wax).

2 Not that potential antecedents need have been exclusively Attic: the mimes of Sophron and the plays of Epicharmus, both Dorian, are as (im)plausible Platonic ancestors as any homegrown Athenian authors.

3 A *very* loose analogy. The Romantics and such as Borges conceive of Shakespeare's achievement as the supreme literary artist (in their eyes) as having something to do with his anonymity, which is supposed to be related to Shakespearian fecundity, energy and weight. So too Plato, by resolutely drawing away from us, attracts most philosophers in his wake. The only remotely comparable experience is to read the works of the late Wittgenstein (you might try *On Certainty*), where the reader must attempt to follow the author's elusive reasoning through unglossed example and counter-example, down false trails and back to uncertain dialectical victories.

4 Translations from Burnyeat 1990. This book cannot be recommended too highly; I do not know of a better commentary on a Platonic dialogue.

5 The Greek lacks our conventions for indicating book titles, so 'the *Truth*' might be 'Protagoras' [doctrine of] truth' (although the editor of the Oxford Classical Text prints a capital letter *alpha*, plumping for the book title). Any which way, Socrates is for the nonce pinning the 'secret' doctrine on Protagoras, retrojecting full-blown relativism leavened with 'Heraclitean' flux onto whatever the nascent Measure doctrine might have been: this is how the tradition of Greek philosophy makes its own history.

6 Why is that? One might think the answer is chronological verisimilitude: we are told in the opening frame that the mortally wounded and ill Theaetetus has just been conveyed back to Athens from battle, and the following dialogue is a record obtained from Socrates of the earlier discussion of knowledge. Thus one might infer that Plato could not plausibly have represented Protagoras as a live participant, because the historical details would preclude such a meeting. But Plato is notoriously happy to play fast and loose with dates (e.g. the encounter between Socrates, Parmenides and Zeno in the *Parmenides*), so that is not likely to be correct. Perhaps we might conjecture that the answer has to do with the relativist's contested claim to be able to participate in dialectic consistently with his principles; that this claim is dubious is expressed dramatically by the need for Protagoras to speak *through* Socrates.

7 Burnyeat 1976a and Waterlow [Broadie] 1977 are the seminal contributions to the burgeoning scholarly literature. Chapter 4 of Passmore 1961, although not so good on the *Theaetetus* itself, is the best place to begin for the type of reasoning at play (and is excellent on philosophical reasoning in general).

8 You may be familiar with Descartes' *Cogito*, 'I think, therefore I am'. What validates this inference? If I think, I either exist or not; if not, then I am mistaken; but if I am mistaken, I must exist to be in error. How the Cartesian argument runs is contentious, but you can see that it seems to exploit the need to avoid self-refutation.

9   The eye of a careless and hasty reader might pass over Theodorus' 'so it appears' as a mere filler line. But remember that Measure states that what appears to X is true-for-X. So this nice touch tells us that it is true (for Theodorus? for you? full stop?) that it is true for Protagoras (or is that qualification now redundant?) that Measure is false. No signs of negligent composition here.

10   Protagoras is not alone. To *The Way of Truth*, in which the goddess reveals the nature of what is, she appends *The Way of Seeming*, wherein she narrates 'deceitful mortal opinions' (the world is a mutable plurality). *The Way of Seeming* is supposed to be a false cautionary tale. But you might ask, if what is is an immutable unity, how could there be foolish mortals at all? How can Parmenides so much as express his theory, without refuting himself? Some scholars, taking their lead from Aristotle, read *The Way of Seeming* as 'an admission of honest perplexity'; others attribute complex dialectical strategies to Parmenides. Plato's *Sophist* formulates two sets of complementary paradoxes, of being and not-being, which make use of self-refutation tactics (something similar happens in the second part of the *Parmenides*). Zeno's paradoxes, on one interpretation, are meant not to vindicate Parmenides' monism, but rather to show that pluralism is no less absurd (nihilistic, universal refutation). Gorgias' *On what is not* argues (or 'argues'?) that there is nothing; were there anything, it would be unknowable; were it knowable, it would be incommunicable – how to communicate *that* message (see Wardy 1996)? There is a fragment of Democritus in which he has the senses complaining to the mind that his theory convicts them of unreliability; but the mind derives its evidence from unreliable perception (most frustratingly, the mind's reply has not survived, so we don't know whether or how Democritus resolved the dilemma). These self-refutation pointers might help you to map out more of the Greek philosophical terrain.

11   After the exchange with Theodorus, Socrates remarks that if Protagoras ' . . . were to stick up his head from below as far as the neck just here where we are, he would in all likelihood convict me twenty times over of talking nonsense . . . before he ducked down

to rush off again' (171D). Why can't the indignant ghost of Protagoras emerge full-length? The interpretation of this grotesque image is contested. But perhaps the dramatic implication has to do with the possibility we are floating, that Protagoras participated in the debate only on sufferance, and that our patient pretence is now to be abandoned. The Greek word for 'convict' here means 'refute': according to whose rules will Protagoras accomplish that? And who is spouting nonsense, if relativism is trying to say the unsayable?

12 However, 183 does allow that there *might* be other ways to defend 'knowledge is perception', which is presumably why at 184 – 6 Socrates refutes the definition independently of the 'secret doctrine'.

13 Owen 1986 contains the most subtle and philosophically sophisticated work ever done on Aristotle's philosophical development (and on much else). Owen is formidably difficult, but philosophy of this calibre is worth the effort.

14 Translations from Kirwan 1971 (whose commentary should be consulted). Use Barnes 1984 for reliable translations of all of Aristotle.

15 The *caveat* clause is added to dispose of the specious counterexamples already scouted by Socrates in the *Republic* (e.g. 'the spinning top is both in motion and at rest'. Yes: in motion, insofar as it is spinning about its axis; at rest, insofar as it is not in rectilinear locomotion. No contradiction.).

16 There is a wrinkle in the translation. Kirwan's 'there would be no *statement* for such a person' might be rendered 'there would be no *argument* with such a person', since his 'statement' renders *logos*. But little hangs on this, since presumably 'there would be no argument with such a person' because he had not said anything.

17 Cf. ' . . . a person reveals his belief in the principle . . . not so much by *what* he says as the fact that he *says* anything' (Lear 1988: 256).

18 Much has been left out, and what is in might be and has been interpreted differently. For example, Jonathan Lear says that 'Heraclitus . . . may sincerely assert that the principle . . . is false' (ibid: 250), since 'Aristotle seems to be focusing on a deeper sense of belief than what an agent thinks he believes. Heraclitus *thinks*

he believes the principle . . . is false, but Aristotle's point is that he is wrong about his own beliefs . . . [he] reveals that he does not know the contents of his own mind' (*ibid*. 251). On Lear's reading, the Aristotelian Heraclitus is strangely deluded; on my reading, the Aristotelian Heraclitus doesn't so much as succeed in *asserting* anything whatsoever, sincerely or otherwise (this and other disagreements notwithstanding, in my opinion Lear's book remains the best available introduction to Aristotle). But, on any interpretation of the argument in *Metaphysics Gamma*, the contrast with the *Theaetetus* stands.

19 I should acknowledge that this interpretation is novel, and reliant on some inevitably controversial assumptions. For example, was Cratylus trying to communicate with others, or just communing with himself? And mightn't it be the case that, by his lights, his finger could successfully follow a moving item, even if that item did not remain unaltered long enough for him to utter anything truly descriptive of it? Needless to say, a Cratylus is not ideally placed to *explain* what he might be up to . . .

3   A life without belief?

1 'Why does he not proceed one morning straight into a well or over a precipice, if there is one about: instead of evidently taking care to avoid doing so, as one who does not consider that falling in is equally a good thing and not a good thing? It is consequently plain that he believes that one thing is better, another not better' (*Metaphysics Gamma* 1008b15 – 19). Aristotle is here chastising an adherent of Protagorean Measure, arguing that his actions belie his words, that they demonstrate he does not really believe that all appearances are true. This is not Pyrrho's doctrine, but shows us how such philosophers were routinely accused of succumbing to the fatal dilemma: consistency spells death; life gives the lie to your pretensions.

2 The differences between the Academics and Pyrrhonian Sceptics, and whether the accusations of dogmatism were justified, are nice

questions: you can follow this up in Long and Sedley 1987 and Annas and Barnes 1985.

3   Despite the 'Pyrrho', the reference is nevertheless clearly to Aenesidemus' neo-Pyrrhonism, not to the obscure historical figure.

4   This information comes from an anonymous ancient commentary on the *Theaetetus*' discussion of Measure; thus we see how our thematic selection is modelled on the tradition's own self-fashioning.

5   In order to exploit the conflicting appearances, the Sceptics used 'modes' for reaching suspension of judgement. These modes – whose complicated history can be studied with reference to LS 72 and Annas and Barnes 1985 – were templates for assembling taxonomical collections of discordant views, including not only philosophical dogmas, but also conflicting human and animal perceptions, customs, predilections and aversions, etc. (Heraclitus and Heracliteans make very useful contributions to the modes, as you would imagine.) Not that the modes were intended to yield truth: as Sextus says, ' . . . I shall make no assertions about either their number or their cogency: it is possible that they are both unsound and more numerous than those which I shall be listing' (LS 72A6).

6   As a last resort, the Sceptic lives in hope: 'when someone presents us with an argument for a thesis which we cannot refute, we reply, "just as before the founder of the school you follow was born the school's thesis did not yet seem sound, but was an objective natural fact, likewise it is possible that the very opposite thesis to the one you have just argued is an objective natural fact but does not yet appear so to us. Hence it is premature to assent to the thesis which appears powerful to us at the present moment"' (from Sextus Empiricus, LS 72A5). This need not be a feeble counsel of despair. Were the Greek philosophical tradition simple and harmoniously static, it would seem evasive wishful thinking to insist that something novel is bound to come along in the future; but such were the unresolved rivalries and endlessly inventive production of argument and counter-argument that it was not at all implausible to deny at any point that the final word had been said.

7   The 'Canonic', or scientific, epistemology of Epicurus provides a curious variant. Since Epicurus was committed to empiricism, he

could not rely on the same criteria for judging all propositions. Sense perception provides direct confirmation of matters of fact accessible to it; but since we cannot perceive microscopic phenomena, in judging between physical theories we proceed indirectly, eliminating such as are 'disconfirmed' by the evidence of the senses (Epicureans maintained that only their atomic theory passes this test). But when it comes to distant celestial phenomena, e.g. eclipses, sensory evidence is insufficient to adjudicate between rival causal hypotheses. The Epicurean response is to accept them all. Their writings seem to shift between the weaker and unsurprising contention that the hypotheses are all equally possible, and the stronger and surprising view that they are all true. However, even on the stronger reading, the Epicureans are not relativists, because their cosmology teaches that there is an infinity of worlds and that time is endless; thus any causal mechanism not 'disconfirmed' is bound to obtain somewhere, some time.

8 A problem for Sceptics: what could justify their claim that tranquillity rather than depression or even despair is the consequence of suspending judgement? They are alert to this issue. All the dogmatic Hellenistic schools promised that the ideal philosopher, the Sage, is tranquil (where 'tranquillity' is a very much more enviable condition than not being fussed). The search after truth is largely motivated by the promise that attaining it in the right way will yield this supreme psychological reward. The Sceptics contend that since this search fails, dogmatists are anything but tranquil. In contrast, once they abandon the futile effort of the strenuous truth-seekers, tranquillity descends on them of its own accord. The painter Apelles failed and failed again to render the effect of a horse's foam; only when he flung his sponge in frustration at the painting did he succeed, by luck (Sextus' *Outlines of Pyrrhonism* I 26 – 9). *Mutatis mutandis* for the Sceptics, who go on calmly searching, neither hopeful nor frustrated. I do not see any grounds for the presumption that this spontaneous serendipity will prove permanent; not that Sceptics are obliged to *fear* the effects of future suspension, but if past experience is no certain guide to the

future, they must remain completely neutral on their future state of mind, which is not too secure a position.

9 I am skirting a controversy. Some scholars (e.g. Burnyeat) think that a Sceptic would suspend judgement on 'honey is sweet' (although, of course, it does appear sweet). Others (e.g. Frede) argue that the Sceptics discriminated between such ordinary judgements and theoretical claims ('honey tastes sweet because its chemical composition affects our sense of taste . . . '), reserving suspension for only the latter. Were this so, where to draw the line between the ordinary and the theoretical? And one couldn't *know* that it was correctly drawn, or wouldn't shift, because that would be a second-order theoretical matter . . . This is a fascinating interpretative controversy, which you can enter by reading Burnyeat and Frede 1997.

10 If the Sceptics didn't suspend judgement on the deliverances of the senses (see last note), and we can now observe the blood's circulation, then it is easy enough to switch to a more recondite medical example.

11 We have now moved some distance from historical Pyrrhonism, as it has come down to us. When Sextus says in *PH* I that a Pyrrhonist is not condemned to inactivity – e.g. he calmly follows a profession – the idea that medical 'expertise' might shift during his practice of it does not seem to have occurred to him (although considerable changes did, as a matter of historical fact, take place). Taking advantage of the *appearance* of efficacity could easily have had a counterpart in ancient Pyrrhonism, but seems to be missing from the record (you will recognise the obvious affinities with Socrates' defence of Protagoras in the *Theaetetus*).

12 I hope you have noticed a family resemblance to Aristotle's refutation of the contradictory Heraclitean. He is supposed to be shown up, once he says anything definite. The Sceptic is not in the same position, since the trap is not sprung if he says, for example, 'the wind seems chilly'; he must say something about how arguments seem to him. But both refutations turn on what it takes to make assertions, any assertion in general, or assertions about the logic of arguments in particular.

13 See Burnyeat 1976b.

Bibliography

Annas, J. and Barnes, J. (1985) *The Modes of Scepticism: ancient texts and modern interpretations*, Cambridge: Cambridge University Press.

Barnes, J. (2nd edn 1982) *The Presocratic Philosophers*, London: Routledge.

—— (1984) *The Revised Oxford Translation of Aristotle*, 2 vols, Princeton: Princeton University Press.

Broadie, S. and Rowe, C. (2002) *Aristotle* Nicomachean Ethics: *translation, introduction, and commentary*, Oxford: Oxford University Press.

Burnyeat, M.F. (1976a) 'Protagoras and Self-Refutation in Plato's *Theaetetus*', *Philosophical Review* 85: 172 – 95.

—— (1976b) 'Protagoras and Self-Refutation in Later Greek Philosophy', *Philosophical Review* 85: 44 – 69.

—— (1990) *The* Theaetetus *of Plato, with a revised translation by M.J. Levett*, Indianapolis: Hackett Publishing Company.

—— (1995) 'Is an Aristotelian Philosophy of Mind Still Credible?', in M.C. Nussbaum and A.O. Rorty (eds) *Essays on Aristotle's* De Anima, Oxford: Clarendon Press.

Burnyeat, M.F. and Frede, M. (eds) (1997) *The Original Sceptics: a controversy*, Indianapolis: Hackett Publishing Company.

Crisp, R. and Slote, M. (eds) (1997) *Virtue Ethics*, Oxford: Oxford University Press.

Guthrie, W.K.C. (1962 – 81) *A History of Greek Philosophy*, 6 vols, Cambridge: Cambridge University Press.

Kahn, C.H. (1979) *The Art and Thought of Heraclitus: an edition of the fragments with translation and commentary*, Cambridge: Cambridge University Press.

Kirk, G.S., Raven, J.E. and Schofield, M. (2nd edn 1983) *The Presocratic Philosophers: a critical history with a selection of texts*, Cambridge: Cambridge University Press.

Kirwan, C. (1971) *Aristotle's* Metaphysics *Books* Γ, Δ, Ε, Oxford: Clarendon Press.

Lear, J. (1988) *Aristotle: the desire to understand*, Cambridge: Cambridge University Press.

Lloyd, G.E.R. (1996) *Adversaries and Authorities: investigations into ancient Greek and Chinese science*, Cambridge: Cambridge University Press.

Long, A.A. and Sedley, D.N. (1987) *The Hellenistic Philosophers*, 2 vols, Cambridge: Cambridge University Press.

Nightingale, A. (1995) *Genres in Dialogue*, Cambridge: Cambridge University Press.

Nussbaum, M.C. and Putnam, H. (1995) 'Changing Aristotle's Mind', in M.C. Nussbaum and A.O. Rorty (eds) *Essays on Aristotle's* De Anima, Oxford: Clarendon Press.

Owen, G.E.L. (1986) *Logic, Science and Dialectic: collected papers in Greek philosophy*, ed. M. Nussbaum, Cornell: Cornell University Press.

Passmore, J. (1961) *Philosophical Reasoning*, London: Duckworth.

Putnam, H. (1975) *Mind, Language and Reality*, Cambridge: Cambridge University Press.

Sandbach, F.H. (1985) *Aristotle and the Stoics*, Cambridge: Cambridge Philological Society.

Sedley, D.N. (ed.) (2003) *The Cambridge Companion to Greek and Roman Philosophy*, Cambridge: Cambridge University Press.

Vlastos, G. (1991) *Socrates: ironist and moral philosopher*, Cambridge: Cambridge University Press.

Wardy, R. (1996) *The Birth of Rhetoric: Gorgias, Plato and their successors*, London: Routledge.

Waterlow [Broadie], S. (1977) 'Protagoras and Inconsistency', *Archiv für Geschichte der Philosophie* 59: 19 – 36.

Index